MEMORA[...]

OF THE PARISHES OF

HURSLEY

AND

NORTH BADDESLEY,

IN THE

COUNTY OF SOUTHAMPTON.

WINCHESTER:

PRINTED BY JA'. ROBBINS, COLLEGE-STREET.

1808.

MEMORANDA

OF THE PARISH OF

HURSLEY,

IN THE

COUNTY OF SOUTHAMPTON.

TO

SIR WILLIAM HEATHCOTE, BART.

THE FOLLOWING

MEMORANDA

OF

THE PARISH OF HURSLEY,

AND

MANOR OF MERDON,

OF WHICH HE IS THE LORD,

Are respectfully addressed,

By his obliged,

Obedient,

And humble Servant,

JOHN MARSH.

Hursley, Aug. 10,
1808.

CONTENTS.

	PAGE
Situation, Extent, &c. of the Parish	1
Proprietors of the Manor	4
Customs of ditto	24
Merdon Castle	31
Cranbury	36
The Church	41
The Vicarage	47
Incumbents on ditto	53
The Parish Register	57
Extraordinary Occurrences	60

Front of the Old Lodge in Hurley Park.

Etched by J. Powell.

MEMORANDA,

OF THE PARISH OF

HURSLEY.

T HE parish of Hursley* lies in the hundred of Buddlesgate, and division of Fawley; and the village is situated on the turnpike-road leading from Winchester to Romsey, and nearly at an equal distance from each of those places.

The parishes by which Hursley is surrounded, are, Sparsholt on the North---Farley on the North-west---Michelmersh and Romsey on the West---Baddesley, North Stoneham, and Otterborne, on the South---and Compton and St. Cross on the East.

The whole parish is upwards of twenty-eight miles in circumference, and contains ten thousand five hundred and ninety acres of land, of which two thousand and six hundred are in common---three hundred and seventy-two in roads and lanes---about one thousand under growth of coppice-wood---and the rest either arable or pasture. .

---

* Formerly spelt Hùrstleghe, from Hurst, a wood, and Lea or Leghe, a place. Locus Sylvestris. See Lambard's Dict. Word—*Hurley.*

B

The soil in the parish of Hursley, as may be supposed in so extensive a tract of land, is of several different sorts: in some parts it is light and shallow, and of a chalky nature; in others, particularly on the east and west sides of the parish, it is what is called *strong* land, having clay for its basis,; and in others, especially that of the commons and fields adjoining, it consists principally of sand or gravel.

Of the Agriculture of the parish I cannot speak particularly, my knowledge of it being imperfect; but it does not, I believe, differ from that practised in other parishes in which the soil is similar. According to the account of Mr. Arthur Young,* who some years since passed through this part of the county, the system of husbandry in use in this parish is, in some instances, peculiarly judicious; but as he was only a passing observer, and in some cases seems to betray a want of accurate knowledge of the practice of the country, I know not whether his observations are entitled to much notice. It ought, however, in justice to be said, that if they are to be considered as good farmers, and as having chosen a judicious course of husbandry, who obtain good crops from an indifferent soil, as, comparatively speaking, that of this parish appears to be, then those of this place have undoubtedly a claim to the distinction of *good* ones; for the crops in general are plentiful, and there is, perhaps, less idle land, in proportion to the whole in cultivation, than might be reasonably expected.

---

* See his " Six Weeks Tour in the Southern Counties, p. 203, 209.

In the year 1781, the number of houses in the parish of Hursley was 227, and that of inhabitants, 1139. In 1795, the inhabitants were found to be only 1099 in number; and in 1801, this number was still farther reduced to 1072. The population of the parish has however, of late, been unquestionably on the increase, and I have no doubt but that at this time, viz. in 1808, it considerably exceeds eleven hundreds.

In the parish, though of so great extent, there is not more than one manor. This is called the manor of Merdon or Marden, and the property of it, until the reign of King Edward the Sixth, had, for many centuries, belonged to the Bishops and Church of Winchester.*

The manner in which they are said to have obtained possession of it, was by the grant of Kinegyls, King of the West Saxons,† who, upon his conversion to Christianity in the year 636, founded a church at Winchester, and gave, for the maintenance of its ministers, all the lands within a circle of seven miles around it.‡ But though Merdon may be considered as coming within this limit, yet it may be doubted, whether the church, at this time, actually became possessed of it; since it appears, by the Annales Eccles. Wint., that it was afterwards given to the church expressly and by name, by Astanus the son of Ethel-

---

* Merdon, I imagine, was one of the Bishop's best manors. It was taxed at the annual value of 80*l.* about the year 1291.—Vide Taxationem Ecclesiasticům, Auctoritate P. Nicholai 4. circa A. D. 1291.

† Kinegyls, King of the West Saxons, began his reign in the year 610, founded the church at Winchester about 636, and died in 641.—Vide T. Rudborne, Hist. Major. Wint. lib. 2, cap. 1.

‡ Vide Rudborne ut supra.

red.*   But whether or not it were in consequence of
the comprehensive grant of Kinegyls, or of the subsequent express gift of Astanus, it is certain that
the manor of Merdon, at a very early date, made a
part of the possessions of the Bishop and Church of
Winchester,† and that it had uniformly so continued
until alienated from the bishopric, as mentioned already, in the reign of King Edward the Sixth.

The person to whom it was then given, and probably at whose instance it was taken from the bishopric, was Sir Philip Hobby, Knt. a man well
known and of considerable eminence as a statesman,
in that reign.   But, unfortunately for his interests, the King did not long survive the grant,
which having been the act merely of his own authority, and never sanctioned by Parliament, was not a
legal, and consequently could not be a secure convey-
ance.   On the accession of Queen Mary, therefore,
Sir Philip, like many others who had acquired epis
copal property, was obliged to relinquish his portion
of it.   Such, however, were the changes in those un-
settled times, that his family soon found itself again
in possession of Merdon: for Mary dying within a
few years after, the former grant was not only renewed by her successor, but confirmed to Sir Philip's

* " Astanus Dux, filius Ethelredi dedit ecclesiæ Winton. duo
Maneria, Merdene et Edgeberi."—Vide Annales Wint. p. 284.
Dugdale, Monasticon, p. 980.

† At this time, the bishop and monks, or ministers of his cathedral, lived together as one family, and the revenues of the church
were the common property of both.   Lanfranc, archbishop of
Canterbury, having separated from the monks and divided their
possessions, his example was soon afterwards followed by all the
other bishops in the kingdom.

son by an act of Parliament, passed in the first year of her reign for that purpose.*

. In a manuscript paper, containing an account of customs and occurrences in the manor of Merdon, written by Richard Morley, who was a tenant of the manor, and born about the year 1576, it is said, that " Sir Philip Hobby was a great warrior—that he " raised his fortune by the wars, and that Merdon " was given to him by a King—that he built the " great lodge, and that he came from Hayles, in " Gloucestershire." Of these statements, the first, I believe, is certainly not true. Sir Philip was often employed abroad as an ambassador,† but was no soldier ; and there is no reason for supposing that his fortune was made by the wars particularly. He had, probably, good interest at Court, and might by such means have procured the grant of Merdon; or it might have been given to him as a reward for his ser-vices, which were important, and gave him a better claim to favour than many others had, who obtained church spoils.‡ As to his building the great Lodge, or Lord's Mansion-house in the Park, this I think highly probable. Until this time, I find no mention made of any other place of abode for the owner of the manor than the Castle, which had now for some years been neglected, and though not suffered to go wholly to decay, was yet by no means calculated for the resi-

---

* Viz. on Feb. 15, 1559. See Rolls of Parliament.

† The following entry appears in King Edward's Journal, p. 26 :— " May 15. Sir Philip Hobbey departed toward France, with ten " gentlemen of his own in velvet coats and chains of gold."—See the Journal in Burnet's Hist. of Reformation.

‡ He was a privy councillor to King Henry the 8th, a zealous Protestant, and a great promoter of the Reformation.

dence of a numerous and wealthy family: and as the bishops had for many years ceased to come hither, it is not likely that they had provided any other habitation. It seems, therefore, far from improbable, that Sir Philip would be induced, by the acquisition of such valuable property, and the advantage of so desirable a situation, to build a mansion here, suited to the wealth and respectability of his family. Whether or not he himself ever inhabited the house which we suppose him to have now built, is a question that cannot at this time be decided. It is most likely that he did not; since, on the restoration of Gardiner to the bishopric, he was certainly dispossessed of the estate;* and as he was then far advanced in age, and was buried within a few years after at Bisham,† the probability is, that he retired and died there, and never more revisited Hursley. It appears, however, that a lady of the name of Hobby was buried in the church of Hursley in 1559; a circumstance from which it may be concluded, that the family was then resident in the parish, and had lost no time in returning to it. This lady's first husband

---

* That the manor of Merdon actually was resumed by the Bishop, and the profits of it carried to his account from this time till 1559, seems evident from the following memorandum entered on the Steward's Roll for that year:—

"1559—Merden. The profits of the manor of Merden, part of the Bishopric of Winchester before this time, were not now brought into the annual account roll, because the said manor, with its appurtenances, by virtue of an act of Parliament held at Westminster the 21st day of January last past, were given and granted to William Hobbey."

Communicated by James Serle, Esq.

† A very costly monument erected to the memory of Sir Philip Hobby and his brother Sir Thomas, by the widow of the latter, may now be seen in the church of Bisham.

was Thomas Sternhold, the worthy translator and versifier of the Psalms, who it is well known was a Hampshire man,* and lived at Slackstead,† a small hamlet in the parish of Farley, within two miles of Hursley. A few lines in praise of his wife, by way of epitaph, written much in his own style, are now to be seen in the church of Hursley, and shall be given in the proper place.

On the death of Sir Philip Hobby, William Hobby, Esq. inherited his father's claim to the manor of Merdon, and soon after the decease of Queen Mary succeeded in securing his right to it, by an act of Parliament passed expressly for that purpose. It is supposed that he was the person who married Sternhold's widow, and that he resided at Hursley. No account, however, of him, or of any events which happened in the parish in his time, has come to my knowledge. His property at Hursley descended to his son Giles Hobby, Esq. who, it appears clearly by the register and other records, was living in the parish very early in the seventeenth century. His last wife was Ann, the daughter of Sir Thomas Clarke, Knt. of Avyington,‡ in Berkshire, to whom he sold the castle and manor of Merdon, reserving, however, to himself and wife, a life-holding in the lodge and park. When this sale was made does not

---

* See Fuller, " Church History, B. 7. p. 406.

† Slackstead was a part of the property of Hyde-Abbey, and had probably been granted to Sternhold by Henry the 8th. In the year 1291, it was taxed at the annual value of 3*l.* 2*s.* 2*d.*—Vide Taxat. Eccles. circa A. D. 1291.

‡ So says the Register, but I suspect *erroneously. Ardington* was the place in which the family of the Clarkes was settled. Sir Edward Clarke, probably the son of Sir Thomas, was High Sheriff of Berks in 1626.

At the time when this transfer was made, Mr. and Mrs. Hobby were still living; but Sir Nathaniel survived them both, and, as it is said in Richard Morley's Manuscript, "had park and all." He built the great stables now standing near the lodge, but resided, I believe, only occasionally at Hursley. At his death, his property devolved to his son Sir Gerard Napier, who was in possession of it in 1635, but how long before that time I know not. In that year, it is said, that a copyhold was forfeited to him as lord of the manor, the owner of it having been hanged for murder,* and that he (Sir Gerard), sold it to other tenants. I have met with no evidence of his having lived at Hursley, and am inclined to think that he never did so for a constancy. He seems, indeed, to have kept his property there no longer than till he could dispose of it to his satisfaction; for in the year 1638, or very near that time, he either sold it to Richard Maijor, Esq. or else exchanged it with him for the manor of Silton, in Dorsetshire.

This gentleman's family came originally from the Isle of Jersey, but he was probably a native of Southampton, his father having been an inhabitant of that town, and also mayor and an alderman of it. Here, by his own account, he lived for some years after purchasing Merdon, having, as it is supposed, lent the lodge at Hursley to his father-in-law, Mr. Kingswell, who lived and died there, and as his grave-stone

---

* This copyhold was recovered by the sister of the criminal, 29 years after, by process at law.—Query. Therefore, whether it may not be inferred from hence, that the copyhold tenements in this manor were not subject to escheat for felony, any more than the gavel-kind lands in Kent?—See Blackstone's Commentaries, vol. ii. p. 84.

shews, was buried in the chancel in 1639. It seems, however, pretty certain that he was himself living at the lodge in or about the year 1645, and that he continued to reside there until his death in 1660. He seems to have been a very shrewd and active man, and never to have lost any opportunity of improving his worldly circumstances; and his sagacity and assiduity were not exerted in vain, for he acquired very considerable property, having, besides his manor and lands in Hursley, a large estate at Chilbolton, and other possessions in the town of Southampton and elsewhere. The love of money was undoubtedly his predominant passion, in gratifying which it is suspected that he was not over scrupulous. It is said, indeed, that even in Cromwell's opinion, his character was not an immaculate one; and if Richard Morley's report may be credited, he oppressed his copyhold tenants grievously.* The latter's memoranda are exceedingly curious, especially where Mr. Maijor is concerned, and shew in some instances that he himself could be no less " *witty*" than he reports Mr. Maijor to have been. " When (says he) " King " Charles was put to death, and Oliver Cromwell " protector of England, and Richard Maijor of his " privy council, and Noll his eldest son Richard mar- " ried to Mr. Maijor's daughter Doll, then Mr.

---

* Richard Morley appears to have been a very extraordinary character. He went to school (he tells us) at Baddesley, to Ralph Blenstone, minister of that parish, in the year of the great hail storm: this was in 1582. Supposing, therefore, that he was then only six years of age, he must have been ninety-six at the time of his death, which happened in 1672. His burial is registered as follows:

" Richardus Morley Senex sepultus fuit Augusti 28°. 1672."

The word *Senex*, being an unusual addition, indicates that he was considered as a very old man.

" Maijor did usurp authority over his tenants at
" Hursley." In another place he says, that " he
" (*i. e.* Mr. Maijor) set forth horse and men for the
" Parliament, and was a captain and justice of peace.
" Lord Richard Cromwell was also a justice of peace,
" and John Dunch a captain and justice. These all
" lived at Lodge together in Oliver's reign; so we
" had justice right or wrong by power; for if we did
" offend, they had power to send us a thousand miles
" off, and that they have told us. When Oliver died,
" Richard was at a great charge for his funeral—
" never had any prince the like. The Londoners left
" to mourn for their money when Richard was turned
" forth. He is fain to keep out of the way, and her
" Highness is come down to live at Hursley upon her
" own land, having left Whitehall to the right King
" Charles 2d."

. The following memorandum may be supposed to
have been written soon after Mr. Maijor's death:
" Mr. Maijor buried the 30th of April 1660. Privy
" councellour to Oliver Cromwell most part of his
" reign.* If he had lived till King Charles 2d had
" called his privey councell he might have chanced
" to have been sent unto them again and advanced
" higher than ever."† He adds, " he was very
" witty and thrifty, and got more by oppressing his
" tenants than all the lords did in 60 years before him.
" He died but a young man to speak of, about 50.
" He had two diseases which the doctors could not

---

* He was also one of the council of state selected by Cromwell in
1653, to manage the civil power.—Dugdale's " View of the
Troubles." p. 406.

. † He means to the *gallows*, I suppose.

"cure.. He had eight issues open upon his body to
" draw the wicked diseases from him. He might
" have cured one of the diseases himself, but he never
" went about to do it; the other was the gout.
" N. B. Was fain to leave the world before he was
" willing, as I think."

By his wife, the daughter of Mr. Kingswell, he
had two daughters only; of whom the eldest, Dorothy,
married Richard Cromwell, Esq. on the 1st of May,
1649, and the youngest, Ann, John Dunch, Esq. of
North Baddesley, in July 1650. The manor and
estates at Hursley were settled upon Mrs. Cromwell
and her issue, and accordingly, on the death of Mr.
Maijor in 1660,* Richard Cromwell became, in
right of his wife, lord of the manor of Merdon. It
happened that he was at this time at Hursley; but as
King Charles the 2d was just then upon his return,
poor Richard could not remain there to enjoy his property. He was born at Huntingdon in 1626, and
though the third by birth, was yet the eldest surviving
son of the Protector Oliver, who sent him with his
brother, to be educated under the eye of his grand-
father, at Felsted in Essex. At the age of 21, he was
admitted a member of Lincoln's Inn, but does not appear to have attended much to his studies, or indeed
to any thing but his pleasures, which, however, there

* In a manuscript paper now in the possession of Sir William
Heathcote, it is intimated that Mr. Maijor hastened his death by
poison—" a dose (as it is there said) being more eligible than an
haltar." But as nothing of the kind is even hinted at by his contemporary, Richard Morley, and it is evident that the writer of this paper
bore no good will either to Mr. Maijor or his family, I am inclined to
believe the surmise to have been as groundless as it was ill-natured;
though it must be confessed that his death happened very seasonably;
a circumstance which might, perhaps, have given rise to the above
mentioned suggestion.

is no reason for supposing were at all of a vicious kind. But leading, as he did, an idle life, his father was desirous of seeing him well settled in marriage, and accordingly procured for him the advantageous connection with Mr. Maijor's daughter. From the time when this marriage took place, which was when he was only 23 years of age, he resided entirely with his father-in-law at Hursley, till the year 1654, when, being elected one of the representatives in Parliament for Hampshire, he lived occasionally in London. Hursley may, however, be considered still as his principal place of abode, his wife having always remained there, and been seldom, if indeed more than once, at the court of Oliver.

On his accession to the Protectorate, he took possession of Whitehall, and there resided during the short period of his elevation. When obliged to withdraw from thence, he retired to Hampton Court, and from thence, probably in the autumn of 1659, to Hursley. Here he continued till towards the middle of the following year;* soon after which he found, or at least judged, it advisable to seek security by retreating to the Continent, where he lived nearly 20 years, as it is said, in poverty, little known or thought of. On the death of his wife, his son Oliver claimed a right, under the marriage settlement of his mother, to the manor of Merdon and estates of her family, and accordingly took possession of and enjoyed them till his death in 1705. But long before this event occurred, Richard was returned to England and resided

---

* It is certain that Mr. Cromwell was at Hursley at the following times after he was Protector, viz. in Oct. 1659, Nov. 1659, May 1660. He was not there in Nov. 1660, and it is thought, not in the July preceding.

at Cheshunt in Hertfordshire, acquiescing contentedly
in his son's pretensions.* Now, however, that his
son was dead, he put in his claim to his former possessions, as his son's heir, and succeeded in establish-
ing it, though not without some opposition ; for his
daughters, considering themselves as the heirs of their
brother, and consequently entitled to his property,
were by no means disposed to relinquish their supposed claim, and it therefore became necessary to
bring the question of right between them, into a court
of law to be decided. In the course of this trial Mr.
Cromwell himself, now in his eightieth year, was
obliged to appear in person. On his entering the
Court, the Judge, who it is believed was the Lord
Chancellor Cowper, struck with his venerable appearance, and probably with the recollection of his
former greatness, received him with the utmost respect, ordered a seat for him, and insisted that on account of his great age, he should sit *covered;* and for
so doing it was said that he was afterwards much com-
mended by Queen Anne. The decision of the Court
proving to be in his favour, he now returned once
more to Hursley, and continued to reside there, principally, during the remainder of his life. But this,
as might be imagined, was a period of no very long du-
ration, for he died within about six years after at
Cheshunt, viz. on the 12th of July, 1712, and was buried
on the 18th of the same month, with his family, in the
chancel at Hursley, having nearly completed the 86th
year of his age. Mr. Cromwell's public character is

---

* If tradition may be relied on, his first appearance at Hursley,
after his return, was in the character of a visiter at one or other of
his tenant's houses, under the assumed name of Clark, which it is
said he used occasionally for some years afterwards.

well known: his *private* one, which perhaps is less so, is concisely, but yet very expressively, and as I believe not less truly given by his contemporary Richard Morley, who says, that "he ("my Lord Richard," as he calls him) was a *very good neighborly man* while he lived with us at Hursley:" and his report is worthy of the more credit, as he was by no means partial to the family, and therefore cannot be supposed to have been prejudiced in Mr. Cromwell's favour.

On the death of Mr. Cromwell, his two daughters succeeded to the estate of their family at Hursley, but kept possession of it only till the year 1718, when they sold it for 36,100*l.* to William Heathcote, Esq. afterwards created a baronet, in the year 1733. Sir William was descended from a family of considerable antiquity and great respectability in the county of Derby, several of whom were, at the end of the century before the last, eminent and wealthy merchants, and well known as leading men in the city of London. He was born I believe at Hackney, in 1693, but losing his father when young, he was brought up under the direction and guardianship of his uncles; the first Sir Gilbert Heathcote, and William Dawsonne, Esq. his mother's brother. The person to whom they entrusted the education of their nephew is not known with certainty, but it is supposed to have been the Rev. Peter Newcome, minister of Hackney; and that the vicarage of Hursley, when vacant in 1727, was given to one of that family, in grateful acknowledgment of the attention and kindness which his tutor had shewn to him.

When about 27 years of age, he married Elizabeth,

Harsley Lodge the Seat of Sir William Heathcote Bt.

the only daughter of Thomas, first Earl of Maccles-
field, then Lord High Chancellor of Great Britain,
on whom and her issue male were entailed all the honours granted to that family. By this lady he had
nine children, viz. six sons and three daughters.-

Sir William was for many years a member of the
House of Commons, having been chosen first to re-
present the town of Buckingham, and afterwards, in
the two first Parliaments of George the 2d, that of
Southampton. The political opinions espoused by
the Heathcote family, at the period of the Revolution,
were those which favoured that happy event, and
placed the House of Hanover on the Throne of this
kingdom. In these Sir William was educated, and
he proved through life a firm, zealous, and uniform
supporter of them : and if it were to this support (as
probably in some degree it was) that he owed the
honour which in 1733 was conferred upon his family,
it must be admitted, by every friend to the religion
and liberty of his country, that his conduct rendered
him not only worthy, but justly deserving of it.

Upon purchasing the estate at Hursley, he began
almost immediately to pull down the old mansion-
house in which Mr. Maijor and the Cromwells had
resided, and to build that which is now inhabited by
his family : but his motive for doing this, was not
that mean and illiberal one which has been most un-
foundedly assigned for it.* The delapidated state
of the old house, with its want of accommodations
for a large and numerous family, were unquestion-

---

* In Noble's Memoirs of the Cromwells, and Guide to a Tour
round Southampton.

D

ably the true and only causes of his destroying it. *

Sir William died in 1751, at the age of 58 years, leaving his title and estates to his eldest son, the late Sir Thomas Heathcote.

Sir Thomas was born in the year 1721, was twice married, and by each wife had four children, all of whom, excepting two, are now living. He was educated at Oxford, and for many years was a Fellow of the Royal Society. No man in any county was ever more generally known, or more popular, than Sir Thomas was in this, in which he lived---his peculiarly amiable and unassuming manners making him not only greatly beloved and respected, but most truly worthy of being so. It was in his time, and chiefly at his expence, as I have understood, that the present parish church was erected: and the family mausoleum, or dormitory, standing in the south-west corner of the church-yard, was also built by his direction. He died in 1787, in the 66th year of his age, and was succeeded by his eldest son, the present Sir William Heathcote.

Sir William was born in the year 1746, was also educated at Oxford, and admitted to the honorary degree of M. A. there, in 1768. In 1790 he was elected by a great majority, though not without a long and arduous contest, member of Parliament for the county of Southampton, and continued the representative of

---

* Since the above account was written, several plans of the old house have been shewn to me by the family, representing the alterations, which it is well known Sir William proposed, had it been found capable of repair, to have made in it; than which, there cannot be better evidence that he did not possess any animosity against the house on account of its former inhabitants.

it during three successive Parliaments. He married Frances, the daughter and co-heiress of John Thorpe, Esq. of Embley in this county, and has had by her eight children; of whom, Thomas, who is now settled at Embley, and member of Parliament for Blechingley in Surry, and who in 1799 married Elizabeth, only daughter and heiress of Thomas Edwards Freeman, Esq. of Batsford, in Gloucestershire, deceased, is the eldest.

CUSTOMS

OF THE

MANOR of MERDON.

THE quantity of land in cultivation within the manor of Merdon or parish of Hursley is, as I imagine, not less than three-fifths of the whole, or about 6000 acres; of which the greater part was anciently copyhold, under the Bishop and Church of Winchester. The tenure by which it was held, was, and indeed is still, that denominated *Borough-English*, the most singular custom of which is, that the *youngest* son inherits the copyhold of his father, in preference of all his elder brothers. The origin of this tenure, according to Sir William Blackstone, is very remote, it being his opinion, that it was " a remnant of Saxon " liberty;"* and was so named in contradistinction to the Norman customs, afterwards introduced by the Conqueror, from the Duchy of Normandy. The reasons commonly assigned for the peculiar usage just mentioned, are given by Blackstone, but they are

* Commentaries, vol. 2, p. 83, 8vo.

evidently not satisfactory to him, and as it should seem, not founded on truth. His own way of accounting for it is far more rational and probable, though it must be confessed, it is only conjectural, He supposes that the ancient inhabitants of this island were for the most part, herdsmen and shepherds; that their elder sons, as soon as they arrived at manhood, received from their father a certain allotment of cattle, and removed from him, and that the youngest son, who continued to the last with him, became naturally the heir of the family and of the remaining property. Whether this were really the case or not, will probably ever remain a question of great uncertainty; and it is a circumstance of too trifling a nature to deserve much investigation. It is, however, worthy of remark, that to this day, this custom of descent to the youngest son, prevails among the Tartars; and that something very like it was anciently the usage among most Northern nations.* But whatever be its origin, or in whatever way it be accounted for, such is the custom now existing in this manor; and I have had frequent opportunities of observing, that it is held, especially by the inferior class of copyholders, as sacred, and that they would, on no consideration, divert their tenements out of the customary order of inheritance.

But besides this custom, there are others also in this manor, which indicate great antiquity, and which, there can be but little, if any doubt, are the same as were in use before the Norman Conquest. We are

---

* See Commentaries, as before.—N. B. Among the Garrows, a people of Hindoostan, the youngest *daughter* inherits the property of her family.—See Asiatic Researches, vol. 3, p. 34. 8vo.

told, indeed, by Judge Blackstone, that after that event, the ancient Saxon system of tenure was laid aside, and that the Normans, wherever they had lands granted to them, introduced the feodal system; and that at length it was adopted generally and as constitutional, throughout the kingdom. There does not, however, I think, appear to be sufficient reason for supposing that this new system was received into this manor, the customs here in use, being evidently those of a more remote age, and in their *circumstances*, if not in their *nature*, altogether unlike those which were at this time established by the Normans.

Under the feodal system, the tenant originally held his lands entirely at the will of the lord, and at his death they reverted to the lord again. The services to be performed for the lord were uncertain and unlimited. The copyhold was also subject to a variety of grievous taxes, which the lord had the privilege, upon many occasions, of imposing; such as aids, reliefs, primer seisin, wardship, escheats for felony and want of heirs, and many more, altogether so exorbitant and oppressive as often totally to ruin the tenant, and rob him of almost all interest in his property.* The difference of the circumstances under which the lands in the manor of Merdon are, and, as it seems, always were held, is remarkably striking: here the copyhold is hereditary---the services are certain and limited---the fines are fixed and unchangable---the lord has no right of wardship---neither is the copyhold liable to escheat for felony---the widow of a tenant has also a right of inheritance---and the tenement may be let without the lord's consent for

---

* Blackstone's Commentaries, vol. ii. chap. 5.

a year. All which circumstances appear to bespeak an original and fundamental difference of tenure from that of the feodal system, and are, I presume, to be considered, not as encroachments that have gradually grown upon that system, but as being of a more liberal extraction and much greater antiquity.[*]
But besides these differences, the supposition here advanced, has this farther ground to rest upon, viz. that neither the name of *Merdon,* nor that of *Hursley,* is so much as mentioned in the great survey of the kingdom, called Domesday-Book, which, if the intention of that survey be rightly understood,[†] it seems next to a certainty that one or other of them would have been, had the new system been here adopted. Nor, when it is considered that this was *Church* property, and that in many instances the alteration was not enforced,[‡] out of favour as it is supposed to the landholder, who was partial to the more ancient tenure, ought it to be thought extraordinary that the customs in this manor did not undergo the general change; since, if favour were desirable and shewn to any, who were so likely to expect and to find it as the clergy? But however this point may really be, it ap-

---

[*] Blackstone's Comment. vol. ii. p. 81, 85.

[†] Sir Martin Wright is of opinion, that Domesday-Book was made soon after our ancestors had agreed to tenures, *i. e.* the feodal system of tenure, for the purpose of ascertaining each man's fee: and he supposes, that as soon as the survey was completed, the great landholders of the kingdom were summoned to London and Sarum to do homage to the King for their landed possessions. Now it may be presumed, that if Merdon had been then surrendered to the King, and any alteration made in the nature of the tenure of the lands in the manor, it would have been reported and registered in the book. But it certainly is not to be found there. May it not then be justly concluded that it was passed over, and that the customs now prevailing are the same as were in use previous to the Conquest?

[‡] See Commentaries, vol. 2, p. 49, 91.

pears evident that the tenants of this manor have, from the earliest times to which we have the means of resorting for information, enjoyed many unusual rights and immunities, and that their services were, in many respects, far from being so base and servile as those of the strictly feodal tenant.

When it was that disputes first arose between the lord and tenants, concerning their respective rights, is not, I believe, known with certainty; but it appears that in the time of Mr. Maijor, many of the lord's claims were complained of by the tenants as usurpations; as on the other hand, many of their's were by the lord, as new and uncustomary. But it was in vain then for the tenants either to resist the lord's pretensions, or to assert their own; such being Mr. Maijor's power and interest with the Cromwellian Government, as to enable him, as they well knew, easily to defeat all their efforts. In justice, however, to Mr. Maijor, it should be mentioned, that he acted in one instance, at least, with great liberality towards the tenants; as by him it was, that the customary personal services were commuted for pecuniary payments, an exchange which could not fail of being peculiarly acceptable to them, as they were not only relieved by it from a service they considered as a grievance, and performed reluctantly, but had the prospect of being in the end great gainers by it. But though by this concession on the part of the lord, some ground of discontent was removed, yet disputes and animosities still continued to subsist with respect to other customs; and no sooner was Mr. Maijor dead, and the Cromwell family dispossessed of its power, than the tenants laid aside their fears, and renewed their opposition. The circumstances of the times being now in their favour, it might, perhaps, have been expected, that they, in their turn, should establish all their claims without contention. The case, however, was quite otherwise; as neither Mrs. Cromwell nor her son would tamely forego any one of their supposed privileges: on the contrary, Oliver defended them in the true spirit of a Cromwell, and relinquished none but such as the decisions of a jury, which were more than once resorted to, deprived him of. In this state of strife and litigation things continued until the year 1692, when most of the principal tenants concurred in a determination to appeal to the Court of Chancery. A bill of complaint was accordingly presented to the Court, stating their supposed grievances, and soliciting its interference. Several hearings and trials, ordered in consequence of this application, for the investigation of the disputed customs, then ensued: after which, though not till more than six years had elapsed, the Court finally adjudged and decreed the customs of the manor to be, and continue for the future, as they here follow:

CUSTOM 1. That all the copyholds and customary messuages, lands and tenements within the said manor are and have been time out of mind, copyholds of inheritance, demised and demisable to the copyholders or customary tenants thereof and their heirs in fee simple, by copy of Court Roll, according to the custom of the said manor.

CUSTOM 2. That the customary tenements within the said manor do descend, and ought to descend, as tenements of the tenure and in the nature of Borough-English, not only to the youngest son or youngest daughter, and for default of such issue of such customary tenant to the youngest brother or youngest sister, but also, for default of such brother and sister of such customary tenant, to the next kinsman, or kinswoman, of the whole blood of the customary tenant in possession, how far so ever remote.

Custom 3. That if any tenant of any copyhold die, seized of any copyhold, his wife living, then she ought to come to the next Court or Law-day, to make her claim and election whether she will pay a penny and hold for her widow's estate, or pay half her husband's fine, and to keep the copyhold tenement during her life.

Custom 4. That the husband of any wife (as customary tenant of the said manor) dying seized of any customary tenement within the said manor, is entitled to have such customary tenement of his wife so dying, during his life, though the said husband had no issue of the body of his said wife.

Custom 5. That if any copyholder or customary tenant of the said manor die, and leave his heir within the age of fourteen years, that then the nearest of kin and farthest from the land, have had, and ought to have the guardianship and custody of the body of such heir and his copyholds, held of that manor, so that at the next Court or Law-day, he come in and challengeth the same, and to keep the same until the heir come to be of the age of fourteen years.

Custom 6. That the heir of any customary tenant within the said manor is compellable to pay his fine to the lord of the said manor, and be admitted tenant before he attain his age of one and twenty years, if he come to the possession of his customary estate.

Custom 7. That the fine due to the lord of the said manor upon the admission or alienation of any customary tenant, to any customary tenement within the said manor, is, and time out of mind, was double the quit-rent of the said customary tenement; that is to say, when the quit-rent of any customary tenement was twenty shillings, the tenant of such tenement did pay to the lord of the said manor forty shillings for a fine.

E

CUSTOM 8. That every heir and tenant of any customary lands of the said manor, may sell his inheritance during the life of the widow of his ancestor, who enjoys such customary estate for her life.

CUSTOM 9. That it is lawful for any of the copyholders or customary tenants of the said manor, to let her, his, or their copyholds for one year, but not for any longer term, without a licence from the lord of the said manor.

CUSTOM 10. That no *certain* fine is payable to the lord of the said manor from any customary tenant of the said manor for a licence to let his customary tenement; but such fine may exceed a penny in the pound of the yearly value of such customary tenement.

CUSTOM 11. That every copyholder of inheritance of the said manor may sell any of his coppices, underwoods, and rows, and use them at pleasure; and may dig for stone, coal, earth, marle, chalk, sand, and gravel in their own grounds to be employed thereon, and may also dig any of the commons or wastes belonging to the said manor for earth or gravel, in the ancient pits therein, where their predecessors have done, for the improvement of their copyholds.

CUSTOM 12. That all the customary tenants of the said manor, when and as often as their old pits where they used to dig earth, marle, chalk, sand, clay, gravel, and other mould, were deficient and would not yield the same for them, that they the said customary tenants may and have used to dig *new* pits in any of the wastes and commons of the lord within the said manor, and there dig and carry away earth, marle, chalk, sand, clay, gravel, and other mould, at their pleasure, for the improvement of their customary tenements, or for other necessary uses, without the licence of the lord of the said manor.

CUSTOM 13. That the ancient customary tenants of the said manor (other than such as hold only purpresture lands) have always had common of pasture, and feedings in all the

lord's commons belonging to the said manor, viz. upon Cranbury Common, Hiltingbury Common, Ampfield Common,
Bishop's Wood, Pit Down, and Merdon Down, for all their
commonable cattle, levant and couchant, upon their respective copyhold tenements within the said manor.

CUSTOM 14. That no customary tenant of the said manor
can or ought to plough any part of the land upon the aforesaid wastes and commons, to lay dung, or for improving
their customary lands.

CUSTOM 15. That the customary tenants of the said manor
have not had, nor ought to have in every year, at all times
of the year, common of pasture in the wastes, heaths, and
commons of the lord of the said manor within the said
manor, for all their commonable cattle, without number or
stint, exclusive of the lord of the said manor.

CUSTOM 16. That the hazels, furzes, maples, alders, wythies, crab-trees, fern, and bushes, growing upon the aforesaid wastes and commons, or in either of them, as also
the acorns when they there fall, do belong to the customary
tenants of the said manor, not excluding the lord of the said
manor for the time being from the same. And that the customary tenants of the said manor have had, and used and
ought to have, right of cutting furzes growing upon the
wastes and commons of the said manor for their firing, and
to cut fern for their uses; and that the said customary
tenants, in like manner, have right of cutting thorns, bushes,
wythies, hazles, maples, alders, and crab-trees, growing
upon the wastes and commons of the said manor, or in either
of them, for making and repairing their hedges, and fencing
of their grounds, but they are not to commit any waste to
the prejudice of the breeding, nursing, and raising of young
trees of oak, ash, and beech, which do wholly belong to
the lord of the said manor, to have, use, and fell; and that
the acorns, after they are fallen, do wholly belong to the
customary tenants of the said manor.

CUSTOM 17. That the customary tenants of the said manor

E 2

have right to feed their cattle in the three coppices, called South Holmes, Hele Coppice and Holman Coppice, within the said manor, and a right to the mast there.

CUSTOM 18. That the lord of the said manor ought not to cut down the said coppices, or one of them altogether, or at any one time, but by parts or pieces, or when he pleases.

CUSTOM 19. That when the lord of the said manor doth cut down any, or either of the said coppices, he, by the custom is not compellable to fence the same for seven years after such cutting, nor to suffer the same to lie open.

CUSTOM 20. That neither Thomas Colson, William Watts, alias Watkins, nor the customary tenants of the tenement called Field-house, have a right of selling or disposing sand in any of the wastes or commons of the lord of the said manor within the said manor.

CUSTOM 21. That any customary tenant of the said manor seized of any estate of inheritance, in any customary tenement within the said manor, may cut timber, or any other trees standing or growing in or upon his said customary tenement, for repairs of his ancient customary messuages, with their appurtenances, and for estovers and other necessary things to be used upon such his customary tenement, without the licence or assignment of the lord of the said manor, but not for building new messuages for habitation.

CUSTOM 22. That no customary tenant of the said manor can cut, sell, or dispose of any trees growing upon his customary tenement, without the licence of the lord of the said manor, unless for repairs, estovers, and other necessary things to be used upon his customary tenement.

CUSTOM 23. That any tenant seized of any estate of inheritance in any of the customary tenements of the said manor, may cut down timber-trees, or other trees, standing or growing in or upon one of his customary tenements, to repair any other of his customary tenements, within the said manor.

CUSTOM 24. That no tenant of any customary tenement of the said manor, may cut any timber trees, or any other trees from off his customary tenement, nor give or dispose of the same, for repairing of any customary tenement, of any other customary tenant within the said manor.

CUSTOM 25. That the said customary tenants, and every of them, may cut down any old trees, called decayed pollard-trees, standing or growing in or upon his customary tenement, and sell and dispose of the same, at his and their will and pleasure.

CUSTOM 26. That the lord of the said manor for the time being, when, and as often as his mansion-house, and the outhouses called *Merden Farm House*, shall want necessary repairs, may cut, and hath used to cut down, one timber tree from off one farm or customary tenement, once only during the life of the customary tenant of such one farm, or customary tenement, for the necessary repairs of the mansion-house and out-houses called *Merdon Farm House*.

CUSTOM 27. That the lord of the said manor, for the time being, cannot cut down more trees than one, from any one customary tenement in the life time of any customary tenant thereof, for the repairs aforesaid, nor can he take the loppings, toppings, boughs, or bark of such trees, so by him cut down, nor can he carry the same away.

CUSTOM 28. That upon any surrender made before the Reeve, or Beadle, with two customary tenants of the said manor, or before any two customary tenants of the said manor without the Reeve or Beadle, no herriot is due to the lord of the said manor, if the estate thereby made and surrendered be from the right heir.

CUSTOM 29. That by the custom of the said manor, the Jury at the Court or Law-day held for the said manor, have yearly used to choose the officers of and for the said manor, for the year ensuing, viz. a Reeve, a Beedle, and a Hayward, and such officers have used, and ought to be sworn at the said Court, to execute the said offices for one year, until they are lawfully discharged.

Custom 30.   That the Hayward's office hath been to collect and pay to the lord of the said manor, such custom money as was agreed for in lieu of the custom-works.

END OF THE CUSTOMS.

The Ruins of Merdon Castle in Hursley Park.

Drawn & Etched by J. Ford.

MERDON CASTLE is situated at the top of the park, and at the distance of half a mile from the lodge, or mansion-house of the lord of the manor. It was built by Henry de Blois, Bishop of Winchester, for the purpose, as it is supposed, of supporting the interest of his brother King Stephen, against the Empress Matilda, mother of King Henry II. The time when it is said to have been erected, was the year 1138; * soon after which (the Empress having taken post in the castle of Winchester) it was more strongly fortified and surrounded with entrenchments.

Being erected on one of the episcopal manors, it became from this time one of the castles or palaces of the see of Winchester; and we have evidence, that it was for many years after, kept in good repair, and habitable for its owners. † It is said, however, to have been suffered to go to decay in the course of the fourteenth century; though, I believe, this was the case with such parts of it

---

* " Anno 1138, fecit Henricus episcopus ædificare domus quasi " palatium cum turri fortissima in Wintonia, castellum de *Merdond,* " et de Fernham, &c." Vide Annales Eccles. Wint. Anglia Sacra, vol. I. p. 299.

† In Bishop Gervays's Account Book, an entry is made of the expence of fitting up the hall in the castle of Merdon. This must have been between the years 1265 and 1268.

It appears from the following passage in the Annales Eccles. Wint. that Nicholas de Ely, Bishop of Winchester, was resident in the castle of Merdon in the year 1278, and that the ceremony of reinstating the Prior of St. Swithin's in his office was then performed there. " Dictus episcopus predictum Valentinum in pristinum " statum prioratus restituit die S. Petri ad Vincula apud Mer- " donam." See Warton's Anglia Sacra, vol. I, p. 314.

only as were intended for defence, and were useless
for the purposes of habitation: for it appears unquestionable, that Bishop Edington resided much
in it in the year 1365; * and there is not wanting
good reason for believing, that some parts of it
were inhabited so late as in the year 1601. At
present, the only remains of the building is a fragment of what is supposed to have been the Keep,
or Dungeon; which, having been more substantially
constructed than the rest of the fortification, has
in some degree, to this day, resisted the destructive
operation of time and weather.

This ruin stands on the north side of the inner
area, and is surrounded by two circumvallations,†
which are still very considerable; and must, when
in a perfect state, have been exceedingly strong.
In the middle of the same area in which the ruin
stands, was, not many years since, a modern farm-
house; but this, excepting a room or two, neces-
sarily reserved for the purposes of the Manerial
Court, was removed by the present proprietor;
and at the same time the whole scite of the castle,
with the intrenchments, was thrown into the park,
and inclosed within its boundary.

---

* See his Register, part the 1st, fol. 129, &c. It appears by
this Register, that in the year 1365, a commission was given by
the Bishop to certain persons, to inquire into a late election of a
prior of Mottesfont, and that the inquiry was directed to be carried
on in the church of Hursley; the Bishop might therefore have come
hither, for the more ready superintendance and dispatch of this
business. At any rate, it seems by the numerous entries in his
Register, which are dated at this place, that he was frequently, if
not for a long continuance, resident here in the year before specified.

† Grose says that these are *concentric*, but he is certainly mis-
taken.

The ancient castle-well, which in depth and diameter was apparently not less than that in the castle
of Carisbrook, * still remains; but at the time the
just-mentioned alteration was made, it was arched
over. The situation of it may, however, now be
seen, and some judgment formed of its magnitude,
a high mound having been raised over it.

On the banks, or ramparts, many trees are now
growing, some of which are of great age, and
highly ornamental—particularly the yews, from one
of which to the west, the eye commands a prospect
of uncommon extent and variety, over Portsdown,
to the high lands of the Isle of Wight, and
towards Salisbury.

The castle continued in the possession of the
Bishops of Winchester, till towards the close of the
reign of King Edward VI; † when, together with
the manor, it was alienated from the see, and
granted to Sir Philip Hobby, Knt. whose descendants kept possession of it till towards the middle
of the seventeenth century.

NOTE.—I have endeavoured to discover, whether or not
the castle was ever besieged, or its strength in any way put
to the proof, as a place of defence; but neither history nor
tradition has been found to furnish any information on the
subject. I am induced therefore to believe, that it never
was of any immediate use in a military point of view,

---

* I have been informed, that the diameter of the well is nine
feet, and the depth of it 300.

† I suppose till the year 1551; this being the year in which
Bishop Gardiner was displaced: for it is concluded, that the lands of
the bishoprick could not be alienated till after he was actually
dispossessed.

F

at least, after the purpose of its first formation was answered.

But though there be no reason for supposing that the castle was ever the scene of any military achievements, yet there are evident proofs that a conflict, and probably a bloody one, was once maintained in the parish. On the common, a mile or two to the south of the village, an encampment of considerable extent is still plainly to be traced, with several (not fewer than eleven) tumuli, or barrows; some of them close by, and others at a small distance only from it. These, I have understood, were not many years since opened, and human bones, with some decayed pieces of iron, apparently parts of ancient armour, found under them. It will be admitted, I suppose, that the persons buried in these places, were on some occasion or other, slain near them. When this occurred can now, I imagine, never be known beyond conjecture. The only battle fought in this neighbourhood, of which we have any account, was that which happened between the Saxons and the Danes in 837. In that year, it is said, that these last appeared in great force near Southampton, and that they were met there by Wolfheard, Ethelwolf's General, who defeated them with great slaughter. As the entrenchments here spoken of, may certainly be considered as near Southampton, and are on the way to Winchester, whither it may be supposed the Danes were marching for plunder, it may seem perhaps not improbable, that they were thrown up on this occasion. There are, however, reasons which rather incline me to think that they are of an earlier date, though I am unable to ascribe them to any one time or occasion in particular. Many of the battles between Cerdic and the Britons were contested in this part of the country. It is agreed upon by all historians that he entered this county at Chardford, near Fordingbridge, and fought his way to Winchester. A stand might therefore have been made against him at this place, which may reasonably be supposed to have

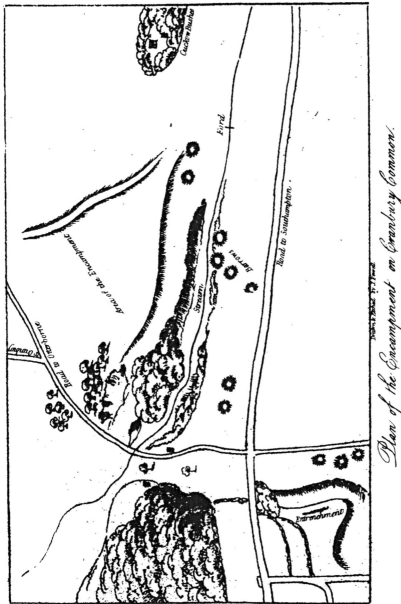

Plan of the Encampment on Cranbury Common.

Croslow Bushes

Ford

Road to Southampton

Area of the Encampment

Barrows

Stream

Road to Crawborne

St Stumps

Entrenchment

lain in his road thither. Should it therefore be conjec-
tured, that these banks were raised on that occasion, the
supposition may seem to have the support at least of
probability.

Mr. Warton would, perhaps, refer them to a still more
remote period;—to the times of the contests between the
Celts and Britons.—See his History of Kiddington.

CRANBURY is situated south-east from the village of Hursley, and at the distance of about two miles from it. It consisted formerly of many distinct tenements, or copyholds; and, it is supposed, was a considerable hamlet : but the name is now appropriated to *one* house only---the property and residence of Sir Nathaniel Holland, Bart.

That there were anciently more houses and families situated at Cranbury, than are now to be found there, seems evident, from the Manerial Court Rolls; in one of which, * the names of not fewer than *eleven* persons are enrolled, as holders of lands within that district of the manor; and there can be no doubt, I presume, but that they were resident upon them.

How long it is since these tenements were united, I am not informed; but there is reason for supposing that many years, certainly not less than two hundred, have elapsed since that time.

Of the proprietors of Cranbury, the first that I find mentioned, was a person of the name of Shoveller; but all that can be now learnt of him is, that he surrendered the estate to Mr. Roger Coram. When this transfer was made is not known exactly,

* The roll here referred to bears no date, but possesses internal evidence of being the account of a year subsequent to 1276. It speaks of the translation (meaning *banishment*) of John Gervays, Bishop of Winton, beyond the seas, and of the 8th year of Nicholas, viz. de Ely.—N.B. The 8th year of Nicholas corresponds with the year of our Lord 1276.

but it was before the year 1580, as Mr. Coram
was then living at Cranbury; and, as it appears,
was resident there for more than thirty years after
that time. From a circumstance or two recorded
of him, he seems to have been a man of great
spirit, and a zealous assertor of the tenants rights
against the lords of the manor. His zeal, however,
on such occasions, can scarcely be considered as
disinterested, since he had several other estates
in the parish besides Cranbury; all of which, except one, were copyhold, and consequently liable
to be affected by the disputes which arose between
the lord and tenants.

On the death of Mr. Coram, Sir Edward Rich-
ards, Knt. appears to have succeeded to the Cranbury property; but the precise time of his coming
into possession of it, has not been ascertained,
neither can it be discovered that he ever lived
there. It is believed indeed, that he resided at
Winchester, and let his house at Cranbury. The
time when he sold the estate was between the years
1640 and 1643.* In the former of these years, he
had been fined the sum of twenty pounds for cutting timber, without a licence from the lord of the
manor for that purpose: and it seems not unlikely
that he was induced, in some degree, by pique at
this exercise of the lord's right over his property, to
dispose of it.

---

* Dr. Young was certainly the owner of the estate in 1643; he
having in that year obtained a license of Mr. Maijor, then lord of
the manor, to let it. The condition upon which the license was
granted was, that the estate should " be let only to a Protestant
" according to the Church of England, and not to a Papist."

The person by whom it was now purchased, was Dr. John Young, at this time Dean of the church of Winchester, and a well known character, He was by birth a Scotchman, and educated in Sidney College, in Cambridge; and had been promoted by King James, in 1616, to the deanery of Winchester. He was also Incumbent of the Rectory of Over-Whallop, in Hants, if not of the Chancellorship, and of a Prebend in the cathedral church of Wells. Considering the times in which he lived, and that he was a churchman, he had no reason to expect favour from the party then uppermost, and it is certain that they did not shew him any; for he was first plundered and driven from his rectory by the rebel army, and soon afterwards deprived of all his preferments by the Parliamentary Commissioners. He then, as it is thought, retired to Cranbury, and within a short time after, died there. The exact year of his death is, however, not known; but as it appears that a Mrs. Young (who, it is supposed, was his brother's widow) was in possession of the estate in 1650, it is concluded that he was then dead, and that he had bequeathed his property to her.

Mrs. Mary Young, the lady just mentioned, was the grand-daughter of Lord Chandos, and widow of Major-General James Young, who was a gentleman of the privy chamber to King Charles the First. This we learn from the inscription on a monument erected to her memory in the cathedral church of Winchester, where she was buried in the year 1687, at the advanced age of 80. How long she lived at Cranbury does not appear; but the probability seems

to be, that she resigned the house to Sir Charles
Wyndham, Knt. on his marriage with her daughter. This marriage was celebrated at Hursley in
1665, and is entered in the parish register in the
following manner :

" Carolus Wyndham Miles, duxit Jacobam Young
Puellam, 19 June, 1665."

Sir Charles Wyndham, who now became the proprietor of Cranbury, was of a most respectable family, being the son of Sir Edmund Wyndham,
Knight Marshal of England, who so zealously supported the cause of King Charles the 1st and 2d in
the west, and suffered the loss of almost all his im-
mense property by his attachment to their interests.*
Nor was Sir Charles less loyal in his principles than
his father, even though the services of his family
were certainly but ill-requited at the Restoration.
He could not, however, it seems, see the arbitrary
conduct of King James, without feeling, what every
friend to his country must have felt---a just resent-
ment, and resolving to oppose it : accordingly in
the Convention, of which he was a member, we find
him concurring in all the great measures of the
Revolution ; and in the two succeeding Parliaments,
in which, as well as in the Convention, he represented the neighbouring town of Southampton, he
appears to have persisted in the same laudable and
potriotic conduct. Having resided at Cranbury
upwards of forty-one years, he died there in 1706,

* See Lord Clarendon's Hist. vol. ii, p. 276.

and was buried in the church of Hursley, near the vestry. His lady survived him many years, and continued to live at Cranbury till her death, which happened in in 1720, soon after which, it was sold to Jonathan Condit, Esq. of whom it was purchased, in or about the year 1737, by Thomas Lee Dummer, Esq. whose son, Thomas Dummer, Esq. succeeded to it in 1765; from whom it has devolved to the present possessor, Sir Nathaniel Holland, Bart.

The Tower of Harsley Church

THE CHURCH OF HURSLEY was become so decayed and ruinous about the middle of the last century, that it was found absolutely necessary to take it down and rebuild it. It is said by those who remember it, to have been extremely low and dark; that the ground on the outside was nearly on a level with the windows; and that the entrance into it was by a descent of six or eight steps. What the form of it was, is not, as I can learn, now recollected; but the scite of it was nearly as extensive as that of the present building, and the roof was certainly supported by pillars, the capitals of some of them being now to be seen in different parts of the village.*

The foundation of the present new church was laid in the year 1752, and the whole building completely finished in 1753. It consists of a nave and two aisles, and is exceedingly neat, light, and airy. In length, including the chancel, it is eighty-two feet and a half, and in width forty-nine, with an arched ceiling, and pillars to support the roof. If it be defective in any respect, it is in height, an addition of which would certainly have been a great advantage to it.

In modern buildings nothing interesting to an antiquary is of course to be expected; little satis-faction is therefore to be looked for by a person of

---

* The ornaments upon these are certainly Saxon, and I have no doubt but that the church was erected prior to the Conquest.

G

this character, in the present church of Hursley. It seems, however, that care was taken, previously to the demolition of the old building, to preserve the monuments and grave-stones which were within it. Of these, the monument erected to the Cromwell family will probably be thought the most worthy of notice. It is of gray or veined marble, in the Doric style of architecture, and is in height thirteen feet, and in breadth nearly nine. The inscription upon it is as follows:

" This Monument

Was erected to the memory of Mrs. Eliz. Cromwell, spinster, (by Mr. Richard Cromwell and Thomas Cromwell, her executors.) She died the 8th day of April 1731, in the 82d yeare of her age, and lyes interred near this place: she was the daughter of Richard Cromwell, Esq. by Dorothy, his wife, who was the daughter of Richard Maijor, Esq. And the following account of her family (all of whom, except Mrs. Ann Gibson, lie in this chancel) is given according to her desire.

Mrs. Ann Gibson, the 6th daughter, died 7th Dec. 1727, in the 69th year of her age, and lies interred, with Dr. Thos. Gibson, her husband, Physician General of the Army, in the church-yard belonging to St. George's Chapel, in London.

Richard Cromwell, Esq. father of the said Eliz. Cromwell, died 12th July, 1712, in the 86th year of his age.

Oliver Cromwell, Esq. son of the said Richard Cromwell, died 11th of May, 1705, in the 49th year of his age.

Mrs. Dorothy Mortimer, a 7th daughter, wife of John Mortimer, Esq. died 14th May, 1681, in the 21st year of her age, but left no issue.

Mrs. Dorothy Cromwell, wife of the said Richard Cromwell, died 5th Jan. 1675, in the 49th year of her age.

Mrs. Ann Maijor, mother of the said Mrs. Dorothy Cromwell, died 13th of June, 1662.

Richard Maijor, Esq. husband of the said Mrs. Ann Maijor, died 25th April, 1660.

Mrs. Dorothy Cromwell, a 5th daughter, died 13th Dec.
1658, in the 2d year of her age.

A fourth daughter died 27th May, 1655, in the 1st year
of her age.

Mrs. Mary Cromwell, a third daughter, died 24th Sept.
1654, in the 2d year of her age.

A son of the said Richard and Dorothy Cromwell, died
13th Dec. 1652, in the 1st year of his age.

Mrs. Ann Cromwell, a 2d daughter, died 14th March,
1651, in the 1st year of her age.

Mr. John Kingswell, father of the said Mrs. Ann Maijor,
died 5th March, 1369."

Near this monument, on the right hand side, is
a stone fixed in the wall, having a coat of arms
carved upon it, the bearings on which are, on a
chevron embattled, between three griffins' heads
erased, three roses; and below, is a brass plate,
with the following lines in old English characters:

" If ever chaste. or honest godly lyfe
Myght merit prayse. of everlastyng fame
Forget not then. that worthy Sternhold's wife
Our Hobbie's make. Anne Horswell cald by name
From whome alas. to sone for hers here left
Hath God her Soule. & deth her lyfe byreft."
         Anno 1559."

Within the communion rails are buried, Mr.
Kingswell, Mr. and Mrs. Maijor, and three of Sir
Charles Wyndham's children; but the inscriptions

upon their grave-stones are in the most customary
form, and in no respect worthy of notice.   That
upon Mrs. Maijor's is here given, merely because it
is nearly effaced, and will soon become, from its
situation, totally illegible. It is as follows :

> Hic jacet corpus Annæ Maijor
> Viduæ Quæ Maritum habuit
> Richardum Maijor de Hursley
> Armigerum et Patrem Johēm
> Kingswell de Marvel Generosum
>   Obiit 13 die Junii Ano. D'ni 1662
>   Ætatis suæ 56.

Leaving the chancel, we come to several stones
lying in a line down the middle of the church, the
first of which covers the remains of a late Vicar,
the Reverend William White, and the next those of
an old Park-keeper,* the inscription on which is in
these words:

" Hic jacet Johēs Bowland qui fuit custos .p.cor'. hor'
de Merdon per quadraginta duos annos et obiit in ffesto Sti.
Clemētis Anno D-ni Milēmo Quadringentesimo Septuagesimo
Quarto.   Cujus anime propicietur Deus."

Besides this prose inscription, there is another to
the same person, in Monkish Latin verse, as follows :

" Hic in humo strat'.   John Bowland est tumulat'.
Vir pius et gratus, et ab omnibus hinc .p.amatus.
Custos .p.cor. prestans quondam fuit hor'.
De Merdon.' quor' et Wintoniæ dominor'.

---

* The Park-keeper seems to have been a person of much respectability. A legacy was left to the Park-keeper of Merdon by
William of Wykeham.—See his Will in Lowth's Life.

Hic quinquagenis.   hinc octenis rite demptis
Cum plausu gētis.   Custos erit in eis.
Festum Clemētis. tempus fuerat Morientis.
M. quadrīgētis annis Christi redimētis
Quadris hiis junctis. simul et cū septuagētis.
Hunc cum defunctis. protege Xte tuis."

These lines are inscribed on a brass plate which
it is supposed was originally, as it is now, affixed to
the wall, as there is not the least appearance of its
having ever been fastened on the gravè-stóne.

Next to the remains of John Bowland, lie those
of Edward Reyner, and Mary his wife; of whom
the former died in 1692, and the latter in 1699.
This Edward Reyner is supposed to have been a very
intimate friend of Oliver Cromwell, lord of this
manor; and there is reason for believing the supposition to be well founded, from the circumstance,
that legacies were left in Mr. Cromwell's will, to
both Mr. and Mrs. Reyner, though neither of them
lived to receive the favour intended for them, Mr.
Cromwell proving the survivor.

At the west end of the south aisle, is a small
marble monument erected to the memory of Sir
Charles Wyndham, Knt. having the following inscription:

" Here lyeth the body of Sir Charles Wyndham, Knt.
And Dame James his Wife, late of Cranbury.
He was the son of Sir Edmond Wyndham, Knt.
Knight Marshal of England.
She was the daughter of Major General James Young,
And grand daughter to my Lord Chandos.
The said Sir Charles and his Wife had
Ten Sons and seven Daughters.

He departed this life July 22, 1706.
She departed this life the 31st of May, 1720.
This Monument
was erected by two of their Daughters,
Frances White and Beata Hall."

Of the seventeen children here enumerated, five, it appears by the register, died in their infancy, and were buried in the chancel at Hursley.

Many other grave-stones may be found in different parts of the church, besides those which are here transcribed; but as they possess nothing to entitle them to particular notice, they are not inserted.

The tower, standing at the west end of the church, is a building of great strength, and considerable antiquity, though it is thought by no means so ancient as the old church. The style in which it is built, is like that in use about four centuries ago. Probably it was erected at the expence of some Bishop of Winchester; and as it is very much in William of Wykeham's manner of building, who was a great repairer of the churches within his diocese,* especially of those upon his own estates, as this of Hursley then was, it seems not unlikely that he was the benefactor. The height of this building is fifty-one feet, and the area within it's walls, a square of nearly fifteen. It contains a set of five bells, which were cast in the year 1713, and an excellent clock lately placed there, the workmanship of an ingenious mechanic of the village.

---

* " Cæterum non immerito memoriæ tradendum est, quod prædictus pater (viz. Willielmus Wickham) ecclesiæ suæ Cathedrali Wintoniensi *aliisque* pluribus locis fecit."—Vide Vitam Willielmi Wickham, per T. Chandler.

The LIVING of HURSLEY was anciently a Rectory, and, as it is believed, wholly unconnected with any other church or parish. Unfortunately, however, for the parishioners, as well as for the minister, it was about the year 1300, reduced to a vicarage, and the great tithes appropriated to the College of St. Elizabeth, in Winchester. The small tithes which remained, being inadequate to the support of the Vicar and his necessary assistants, the church of Otterborne was consolidated with that of Hursley,* and the tithes of that parish, both great and small, were given to them to make up a sufficient maintenance; an arrangement which, in that dark age, was thought not only justifiable, but even laudable; but which, nevertheless, deserves to this day to be severely censured; since not only the Minister, but both the parishes and the cause of Religion, have suffered a serious and continued injury from it.

The person by whom this appropriation was made, was John de Pontissera, alias Points, Bishop of Winchester, the founder of the College to which the tithes were granted; it was, however, afterwards confirmed by William de Edington, by whom the Vicar's

---

* There appears, I think, very satisfactory evidence that the church of Otterborne was a separate and independent church about the year 1100: I suppose it therefore to have been now first consolidated with that of Hursley, because I know not when, or on what other occasion, it could have been annexed to it. But as there is room for a difference of opinion as to this fact, I would not be understood to speak positively.

rights, which before were probably undefined, and perhaps the subject of contention, were ascertained and secured to him by endowment. This instrument is still in being,* bearing the date of 1362, and the following is a translation of it, so far as the vicar's interests are concerned in it : " The said Vicar shall
" have and receive all and all manner of tithes, great
" and small, with all offerings and other emolu-
" ments belonging to the Chapel of Otterborne,
" situated within the parish of the said Church (viz.
" of Hursley). He shall also have and receive all
" offerings belonging to the Church of Hursley, and
" all small tithes arising within the parish of the
" same, viz.—the tithes of cheese, milk, honey, wax,
" pigs, lambs, calves, eggs, chicken, geese, pigeons,
" flax, apples, pears, and all other tithable fruits
" whatsoever of curtilages or gardens. He shall
" also receive the tithes of mills already erected, or
" that shall be erected. He shall also receive and
" have all personal tithes of all traders, servants,
" labourers, and artificers whatsoever, due to the
" said church. The said Vicar shall also receive
" and have all mortuaries whatsoever, live and
" dead, of whatsoever things they may consist. The
" said Vicar shall also receive and have all profit and
" advantage arising from the herbage of the church-
" yard. He shall also have and receive the tithes of
" all fish-ponds whatsoever, within the said parish,

---

* It may be seen in Bishop Edington's Register, part i, fol. 128, under the following marginal title:—" Ratificatio et Confirmatio " appropriationis Ecclesiæ de Hursleghe, et ordinationes Vicariæ " ejusd."

" wheresover made, or that hereafter shall be made;
" The said Vicar shall also have for his habitation,
" the space on the south side of the church-yard,
" measuring in length from the said church-yard and
" the rectorial-house, formerly belonging to the said
" church, towards the south, twenty-seven perches;
" and in breadth, from the hedge and ditch between
" the said space and the garden of the aforesaid for-
" mer rectory on the west, towards the east, sixteen
" perches and a half, with the buildings erected
" thereon,"

Besides the above, John de Pontissera allotted to the Vicar the tithes of wool, beans, and vetches; but of the first of these he was deprived by Bishop Edington's endowment; and the latter have been so little cultivated, that he has never yet derived any advantage from them, though his right to this species of tithes cannot, I suppose, be questioned, unless, indeed, they are comprehended under the term *Bladum*, and are consequently to be considered as the portion of the Impropriator.*

The church of Hursley is situated within the Deanry of Winchester, and is a Peculiar; a distinction which it enjoys, probably, in consequence of its having been formerly under the patronage of the Bishop. The advantages of this are, that it is not subject to the Archdeacon's jurisdiction; that the Minister is not obliged to attend his Visitations; and that he has the privilege of granting letters of

* The tithes given by the Endowment to the President and Chaplains of St. Elizabeth College, are—" Decimæ Bladi cujuscunque " generis, Fœni ac Lanæ," and no other.

H

administration to wills, when the property conveyed by them lies within the limits of the Vicarage.

The value of the Benefice, as rated in the King's Book, is 9*l.* per annum,* and the tenths are of course 18*s.* These the Incumbent is required to pay annually, but he is exempted from the payment of First Fruits. The land-tax with which the Vicarage is charged is 14*l.* 1*s.* 2½*d.* per annum ; and the procurations and diet-money payable on account of the Bishop's Visitation amount to 12*s.* 9½*d.*

The patronage of the Living, when a Rectory, belonged to the Bishops of Winchester, and afterwards, when reduced to a Vicarage, was expressly reserved to himself and successors by William de Edington; and so long as they kept possession of the Manor of Merdon, they continued Patrons of the Vicarage: for the same act of the Legislature which dispossessed them of the one, deprived them also of the other. As it may be supposed they were both granted to the same person, and what is perhaps a little remarkable, they have never since, or indeed at any time, been separated.

During the time the Vicarage was sequestred by the Parliament in the great Rebellion, all the rents

---

* In the year 1291, the Vicarage of Hursley was rated, in what is called Pope Nicholas's Valuation, at the sum of 46*l.* 13*s.* 4*d.* per annum. But though it is there styled a Vicarage, I am inclined to think that the whole of the tithes, both great and small, were included in the estimate; and I am the rather of this opinion, as there is good reason for believing, that the appropriation to Elizabeth College had not then been made.

In 1405, the revenues of the Church of Hursley, cum Capella, were valued at 70*l.* 4*s.* per annum. But the annual value returned in 1529, amounted to only 9*l.* at which rate it has ever since continued in the Liber Valorum.

and emoluments of it were received by Richard
Maijor, Esq. then lord of the manor of Merdon,
and he both provided and paid the Ministers who
performed the duties of the churches. His account
of the receipts and expences, which appears to be a
very correct and just one, commences at Christmas
1645, and reaches to Michaelmas 1649. For the
first half-year there seems to have been no settled
Minister ; payments having been made to no fewer
than seven different persons " for travell and paines
" in preachinge," within that period. But from
Midsummer 1646, to Michaelmas 1649, Mr. Robert
Webb and Mr. Daniel Lloyd appear to have been
settled upon the Cures, the former at Hursley and the
latter at Otterborne. Whether they continued their
" paines" beyond that time I know not ; but as their
stipends were small, they had no great reasons for
remaining; and as the name of John Tabor is not
long afterwards mentioned in the Register as Minister
of the Parish, I conclude that they withdrew to better
preferment.* Nor was this last person's stay of any

---

* It appears that the Puritanical Divines were not altogether so
disinterested in the cause of Religion, as their professions of zeal " for
" the good of souls," might induce us to expect; on the contrary,
we find that they sought the best Benefices with the utmost solici-
tude, and were not content unless they had two or three, and in
some instances *four* of them a-piece. Dugdale tells us, that an
Assembly-man, being informed by an eminent person, that a church
in the west was without an Incumbent, immediately inquired the
value of it, when finding by the answer, that it was only 50*l.* per
annum, he replied—" If it be no better worth, no Godly-man will
" accept of it." And it is a truth well known, that where the
Benefices were very small, the church doors were seldom opened.—
See Dugdale's View of the Troubles, p. 225.

H 2

longer continuance, since it appears that he was succeeded by Mr. Walter Marshall, in 1657.

During the short period in which Mr. Maijor had
charge of the Vicarage, the receipts amounted to
366*l*. 1*s*. 8*d*. and the expences to 362*l*. 15*s*.   After
Michaelmas 1649, the rents of the Benefice were,
as I imagine, received by the Minister himself.

THE

THE following Catalogue of the Incumbents of Hursley has been collected, chiefly, out 'of the Registers of the Diocese, and is perhaps as complete and correct a one as can possibly now be given :

. John de Raleghe was Rector of Hursley, and died in 1279. The time of his collation could not be ascertained; but if he were a relative of the Bishop of that name, and collated by him, as it may be presumed he was, it must have been before the year 1250.

Paganus de Lyskeret, styled Presbyter, was collated in 1280. It appears that at this time there was a perpetual Vicar established in the Church of Hursley, as well as a Rector; and that he was instituted by the Bishop, had a certain fixed maintenance assigned to him, and was independent of the Rector. In the Register of John de Pontissera, Bishop of Winton, may now be seen what is there called the "Ordinatio Episcopi inter Rectorem et Vicarium " de Hurslegh." It is therein settled, that the Vicar shall have a house as described, and other emoluments, and that the Rector shall pay to him forty shillings per annum. The Vicar at this time was Johannes de Sᵗᵃ· Fide. The deed of settlement was executed in Hyde Abbey, in the year 1291: Philip de Barton, John de Ffleming, William de Wenling, and others being witnesses to it. Vide Regist. de Pontissera, fol. 10.

Hugo de Welewyck, styled Clericus, succeeded in 1296, on the resignation of Paganus, and was the last Rector, the Benefice having in his time been reduced to a Vicarage, by the appropriation. of the rectorial-house, tithes, and .glebe, to the College of St. Elizabeth. The *pretences* assigned for this act, for true *reasons* they could scarcely be, since in all cases of appropriation and consolidation, they appear to have been almost exactly the same, were the unfinished state of the college buildings, and the insufficiency of the revenues for the maintenance of the society, owing to wars, sickness, pestilences, and the like. But notwithstanding this serious deprivation and loss, a Vicar it appears was still continued in the church, Hugh de Welewyck having presented two, viz. Henricus de Lyskeret, in 1300; and Roger de la Vere in 1302; of whom the latter was certainly appointed after the appropriation.

William de Ffarlee was collated Vicar of Hursley, on the death of Welewyck in 1348.

William de Middelton was collated in 1363. It was during his incumbency, that the appropriation to St. Elizabeth College was finally ratified, and the Vicar's rights defined and settled. Vide Registrum de Edyngton.

Thomas Cove became Vicar in 1392. He was a native of Winchester, and educated in the College then lately founded there by William of Wykeham.

Walter Cowper succeeded by exchange with Cove for Alton, in 1412.

John Langshaw was collated by Cardinal Beaufort, but in what year cannot be ascertained. Before 1447,

William Emery succeeded by exchange with J. Langshaw for Sutton Waldron, in 1454.

John Lovyer became Vicar of Hursley in 1482. He was a native of Stockbridge, and a Fellow of New College in Oxford.

William Capell is supposed to have succeeded next, as he was Vicar in 1529; but the year of his collation could not be discovered.

John Hynton appears to have been Vicar in the time of Bishop Gardiner; but whether he was the immediate successor of Capell or not, is uncertain. Being a Papist, and refusing to renounce his errors, he was deprived in 1565.

Richard Foxe was instituted in the same year, on the presentation of William Hobby, Esq.

William Symmons, on the presentation of the same William Hobby, Esq. was instituted in 1581. He died and was buried at Hursley in 1616.

John Cole was instituted in 1616. He was a native of Winchester, and a Fellow of New College in Oxford; which he quitted on being promoted to the Vicarage of Hursley. He was also Rector of Michelmersh, but resided at Hursley, where he died and was buried in 1638.

John Hardy was instituted in the same year, on the presentation of Gerard Napier, Esq. but enjoyed his benefice only for a few years, having been dispossessed of his rights by Mr. Maijor, and obliged to withdraw from the parish *; and as he was not replaced at the Restoration, it is supposed that he was then dead. From the time of Mr. Hardy's removal, Mr. Maijor took upon himself to provide for the due serving of the churches, and appears to have been by no means inattentive to his undertaking; though not being very liberal in his payments, he seems at first to have found some difficulty in procuring a Minister to settle upon the Cure. Out of the great variety of those by whom the churches were supplied during the Usurpation, the only one of any repute was

Walter Marshall. He had been a Member of New College in Oxford, and in the year 1657 was elected to a Fellowship in that near Winchester; but whether he had been educated in this latter College, I am not informed: I rather think he had not, and that he had been intruded into New College in the year 1647, by the parliamentary visitors; almost all the members of that society having been then expelled on account of their loyalty. By the parish register it appears, that he was settled at Hursley, as the

---

* This appears from the following entry in the Parish Register—
" 10 Nov. 1644, Johannes fil. Johannis Hoare, baptizatus fuit apud
" Badsley pro defectu Curati in Hursley, in tempore belli."
Mr. Hardy is not mentioned by Walker, in his Account of the Suffering Clergy.

Minister of the Church, in the year 1657; and it is supposed that he continued there till 1661; in which year he resigned his Fellowship of Winton College, and retired to the town of Gosport. He was the author of a Treatise on " The Gospel Mystery of Sanctification;" a work certainly of some merit, and which was republished in 1761, with a recommendatory Preface, by Mr. Hervey, of Weston Favell.

Robert Maunder was instituted in 1660, but on whose presentation does not appear. He died at Hursley, at the age of 71, and was buried in the chancel, where his grave-stone may now be seen, lying contiguous to the Cromwell monument.

Thomas Pretty was instituted on the death of Maunder, in 1673, on the presentation of Oliver St. John, Esq. who, it is supposed, had purchased this turn of Mrs. Cromwell. He resigned.

Matthew Leadbeater was instituted in 1684, on the presentation of Oliver Cromwell, Esq. He was also Rector of Houghton, whither he removed and died.

Edward Griffiths was instituted on the death of Leadbeater, in 1707.

Richard Newcome was instituted in 1726, on the presentation of William Heathcote, Esq. He resigned in 1747, became a canon of Windsor, and was afterwards promoted to the Bishoprics of Landaff and St. Asaph.

William White, on the resignation of Dr. Newcome, was instituted in 1747, on the presentation of Sir William Heathcote, Bart.

Samuel Gauntlett, Fellow of Winchester College, was instituted in 1780, on the presentation of Sir Thomas Heathcote, Bart. He was elected Warden of New College, in Oxford, in 1794, and resigned the Vicarage in 1804.

Gilbert Heathcote, Fellow of Winchester College, succeeded in the same year, on the presentation of Sir William Heathcote, Bart. and is the present Vicar.

THE REGISTER of the Parish of Hursley was begun in the year 1600, and has been very regularly kept from that time to the present, except from the year 1716 to 1722, in which period no entry was made of any burial; nor do the baptisms appear to have had much more notice taken of them, not one being registered between the years 1714 and 1718. The reason of this long neglect I have never been able to discover, unless it be, as I have understood was the case, that there was no Minister resident in the parish at this time. Previous to the year 1664, the entries in the Register were, for many years, not made by the Minister, as had been usually done, but by a person chosen and sworn to the office of Register-keeper, as appears by the following memorandum, to be found at the beginning of one of the books :

" The two and twentieth day of September, anno domi-
" ni 1653, John Wool, of Hursley, was elected and chosen
" Parish Register of Hursley and Otterborne, and sworne
" for the true executing thereof.
Before me, Ric. Cromwell."

Whether this practice was peculiar to this parish, or to that particular time when most ancient usages were discontinued, I know not; but justice requires it to be observed, that the Register does not appear to have been ever more regularly and carefully kept, than within the period here alluded to.

I

The Maijor and Cromwell families being at this time at their height of power and grandeur, the Register-keeper seems to have thought the occurrences in those families entitled to some mark of respect and distinction; he has accordingly entered them at the beginning of the book, separately from the general register of the parish. As it is curious to see Richard's progressive advancement to titles and honours, according as his father Oliver rose to them, a copy of a few of the entries in this part of the book is here given.

Births.

Mrs. Elizabeth Cromwell, the daughter of the Right Worshipfull Richard Cromwell, Esq. by Mrs. Dorothy Cromwell, his wife, was borne * the 26th day of March, anno dom. 1650.

Mrs. Anne Cromwell, the daughter, &c. (as above) was borne the 15th day of July, 1651.

Mrs. Marie Cromwell, the daughter of the Right Houourable the Lord Richard Cromwell, by the Ladie Dorothy Cromwell, his wife, was borne the 18th day of February, 1653.

Oliver Cromwell, the sonne of the Right Honourable the Lord Richard Cromwell and the Ladie Dorothy Cromwell, his wife, was borne the 11th day of July, 1656.

The Ladie Anne Cromwell, the daughter of his Highness Richard Lord Protector of the Commonwealth of England, Scotland, and Ireland, by the Ladie Dorothy Cromwell, his wife, was borne the 27th day of March, 1659.

---

* N. B.—The *Birth*, not the Baptism, of the children is here registered. This was done in conformity with an ordinance, voted by Cromwell's Great Council, appointed to manage the civil power, reform abuses, &c. &c.—See Dugdale's View of the Troubles, p. 410.

Mrs. Dorothy Cromwell was borne the 1st day of August, anno domini 1660.

That a judgment may be formed of the present increased population of the parish, a statement of the numbers of Baptisms, Burials, and Marriages, during three detached periods, is here added from the Register, viz,

	BAPTISMS.	BURIALS.	MARRIAGES.
	No.	No.	No.
1st Period. From 1691 to 1710, inclusive	380	291	62
2d. From 1741 to 1760, inclusive	576	396	95
3d. From 1781 to 1800, inclusive	738	430	136

From the above statement, it may, I suppose, be reasonably concluded, that the present number of inhabitants is nearly double what it was a century ago.

I 2

EXTRAORDINARY OCCURRENCIES, &c.

1582.—A great hail storm happened at Hursley, Baddesley, and in the neighbourhood, this year. The hail-stones measured nine inches in circumference.

1604.—The plague made its appearance at Anfield. It broke out in November, and continued till the following February. Many persons died of it, and were not brought to the church, but buried in the waste near their residence.

1610.—A person of the name of Wooll hanged himelf at Gosporte, in the parish of Hursley, about this time. He was buried at the corner of Newland's Coppice, and a stake was driven through his body.

1621.—A planked thrashing-floor first laid down in the parish in this year, viz. at Merdon. Chalk-floors used before.

1629.—A great fall of snow in October. It was nearly half a foot deep, and remained on the ground three or four days.

1635.—A copyholder was hanged for murder this year. His copyhold seized by the lord as forfeited, but afterwards recovered, viz. in 1664.

1650.—The chalk-pit at Hatch-gate first opened about this time.

1658.—The greatest quantity of snow that had been known for 50 years, fell this year, in January, and lay on the ground six weeks. The thaw came at last with a north wind; and when the snow melted, as it did suddenly, the water ran down Hursley-street, and filled all the cellars.

1666.—The plague appeared again at Hursley in this year, viz. at Longmore. The names of sixteen persons who died of it, are entered in the register. Of this number, five were of the Doling family, viz. father, son, and three daughters. They were all buried at Longmore, except one, who dying as it is supposed at Silkstead, was buried there.

1775.—After a series of wet years, the springs of the parish became so abundant about this time, as to break out, and nearly to fill all the wells and cellars in North-End and Hursley-street; and the old people of the parish then remembered, that a similar event had happened about half a century before.

NOTE.—Mr, Milner, in his History of Winchester, vol. 1, p. 111. tells us, that the Saxon King Kenwulph was assassinated in the village of Merdon, meaning by " the vil-" lage of Merden," the village of Hursley; Merden or Merdon being the name of the manor lying within the parish of Hursley,

As this event had never before been appropriated to this place, and Mr. Milner's assertion is in direct opposition to the generally received opinion as to the scene of Kenwulph's death; it was of course to be expected, that some good evidence should be produced in support of it. So far, however, from finding, in the authors he refers to, sufficient ground for a *positive assertion*, I scarcely can see enough even for a conjecture.

The writer, whose authority he appears principally to rest upon, is Rudborne; who says, that the King was killed " in villâ quæ Meritonâ dicitur," in a village which is called Meritona, i, e, which was so called at the time when he was writing.

Now even upon the supposition that the word Meritona. should be here used to signify Merdon, yet it can scarcely be thought that this place could have been intended, since it is certain that this village was not called Merden in Rudborne's time, and not likely that it ever bore that name at any time.

Hursley, or Hurstleghe, as it was anciently spelt, is well known to be a name of Saxon origin; and there cannot be a question, I imagine, that this parish, so long perhaps as it has been a parish, has gone by it, and by no other. In Rudborne's time it certainly did go by it, and for many centuries before, as is evident from the registers of the diocese, with which he, as an Historian, must have been acquainted; and it is probable, that it was not known generally *then*, any more than it is *now*, that the parish had any such name as Merdon in any way connected with it. Had Rudborne, therefore, meant to speak of *this*, as the place where Kenwulph was killed, it is no more than reasonable, I think, to suppose, that he would have given it its *usual* and *proper* name, and not one which it certainly did not then, or perhaps ever, bear.

It may be objected farther to Mr. Milner's assertion, that if Rudborne really did intend to speak of Merdon, *i. e.* of this manor, he would have used the Latin word, which, in his time, was known, and commonly employed to denote it, which, however, he has not done. In the Annales Eccles. Wint. viz. ad annos 1138 and 1271, the name given to Merdon in Latin, is Merdona; and in all the Rolls of the Manor Court, and other ancient records written in that language, the same word is uniformly used to express it. Why, then, may it be asked, should Rudborne, if he intended to speak of this manor, employ a different word—and a word, too, which he must have well known was generally used to designate another and very different place? Certainly no reason can be assigned for his doing so; and we are consequently justified in concluding, not only that

Meritona was not the Latin name for this manor, but that it was not used by this writer to denote it.

Mr. Milner's error (for such I think it is) seems to arise from the supposition, that it was *near Winchester* that the tragical event happened; but for this there appears to be no foundation in Rudborne, any more than for the assertion, that Kynehard " lay lurking in the woods near that " city."

It may be observed, too, that though Mr. Milner, in his Index, speaks of Hursley as the scene of this catastrophe, yet in his Note to the account, he places the event at Merden, *near* Hursley, as if there were a village of that name different from Hursley; which, however, he might have known was not the case; and that at the time he is speaking of, and for many centuries after, there was not even a castle, at the place he seems to allude to.

According to Camden, and other respectable writers of the same character, Merton, in Surry, is the place at which Kenwulph was murdered. But the truth is, that though Merton was certainly the name of the place at which the fatal event occurred, yet there is nothing in any of the ancient historians to fix it to Merton in Surry, more than to any other place of the same name in any other southern county; unless, indeed, the circumstance, that Sigebert, the predecessor of Kenwulph, lost his life by the hands of an assassin not far distant from that place, may make it probable, that the same neighbourhood might be fatal to both of them.

THE END.

MEMORANDA

OF THE PARISH OF

NORTH BADDESLEY,

IN THE

COUNTY OF SOUTHAMPTON.

TO

SIR NATHANIEL HOLLAND, Bart.

THE FOLLOWING

MEMORANDA

OF THE

PARISH AND MANOR

OF

NORTH BADDESLEY,

OF WHICH HE IS THE LORD,

Are respectfully addressed,

By his obliged,

Obedient,

And humble Servant,

JOHN MARSH

MEMORANDA

OF THE PARISH OF

NORTH BADDESLEY,

THE parish of North Baddesley lies in the hundred of Mainsbridge, and is situated at the distance of three miles, nearly East, from the town of Romsey; at the same distance, to the South-west, from the village of Hursley; and at about six miles, nearly North, from the town of Southampton.

The parishes contiguous to it are, Hursley on the North; Romsey on the West; Chilworth on the South; and North Stoneham on the East.

The whole parish is thought to be between eight and ten miles in circumference, and to contain about two thousand acres of land, not much more than one half of which, it is supposed, is in cultivation, the rest being either woodland or common.

The soil in the parish of Baddesley, like that of most other extensive parishes, varies considerably. In some parts, it consists of strong clay; in others, of a clayey loam; and in others, of that which is peculiar to the production of heath. Till of late years, but little corn was sown in the parish, the land being exceedingly springy and unfavourable to the growth of it; but by draining, which is now practised generally by all the farmers, the soil is rendered dry and productive of grain of all kinds. The manner in which this operation is performed, is so cheap and simple, that it ought to be described. Having digged a trench about three feet deep, it is first filled up, nearly half-way, with stones loosely thrown in; upon these a thick covering of heath is laid, and then the earth is shovelled in till it is level with the surface. The drains thus made, are found to answer the intended purpose, perfectly, for about ten or twelve years, but not longer; as by the end of that time, they are generally choaked up and useless. Chalking is also much in use in the parish, and proves of the utmost utility, by correcting the tenacity and crudeness of the soil. The quantity usually laid on is ten tons to an acre. This being spread over the land, is permitted to remain on the surface during two years, or at least winters; when it is ploughed in, and is found to have a beneficial effect for six or eight years.

What course of crops is observed in the parish, I am not well informed; but if a judgment may be formed from the appearance of the crops themselves, which are usually abundant, it must be judicious and well chosen.

The number of families now in the parish is forty-four, and that of inhabitants two hundred and thirty.

Judging from the register of Births, &c., I should imagine the population to have been much larger about a century ago, than it is at present ; as the entries were then by far more numerous than they are at this time.

The whole parish constitutes only one manor, in which, as I have understood, the number of land-holders was formerly considerable ; but the tenure being for lives only, many of the estates so held, have, of late years, fallen into the lord's hands, and there are now, not more than four or five remaining.

The earliest record which I have met with, and, probably that can be found of the parish, is that given in the ancient survey of the kingdom, called Domes-day Book, and which is as follows : " Ipse " Radulphus (viz. de Mortemer) tenet Bedeslei. " Cheping tenuit de rege. Tunc et modo se defen- " debat pro 2 hidis. Terra est 4 carrucatæ. Ibi " sunt 4 villani et 7 bordarii cum 2 carrucatis et 7 " servi. Ibi æcclesia et silva de 10 porcis ; et pro " herbagio 10 solidi. T. R. E. valebat 10 libras, et " postea 100 solidos ; modo 60 solidos." *

---

* See Hampshire, from Domes-day Book," p. 169.

In the British Museum is a small manuscript paper, which is de-scribed in the Index or Catalogue, as " The History of Baddesley in Verse." It is in the Cotton Collection, and consists of twenty lines only, of which the following are the two first :—

" This seate and soyle from Saxone Bade, a man of honeste fame,
" Who held it in the Saxon's time, of Badesley took the name."

At first sight, I had no doubt but that Baddesley in Hampshire was the place intended, the description, in several instances, an-swering to it. It must, however, be confessed, that it does not agree throughout ; and that it seems, on the whole, to suit Bad-desley Clinton, in Warwickshire, better than this place. But quære,

From this description, it appears that the parish
of Baddesley previously to the Norman invasion,
was possessed by a person of the name of Cheping,
but that it soon afterwards became the property of
Ralph de Mortemer. Who Cheping was, and how
he came to be deprived of his possessions, I know not,
nor have any means of learning; but the probability
is, that he had espoused the cause of the invader's
unfortunate competitor, and that his estates, which
it is very evident, from Domes-day Book, were very
extensive, were on this account confiscated. Ralph
de Mortemer, to whom they were afterwards granted,
was a Norman Baron, nearly related to William, and
one of the most renowned warriors of his time.*
He had accompanied his relation in his expedition
to England, and made himself exceedingly useful
to him on that occasion. But the service which
gave him the best claim to the Conqueror's favour,
was his having been successful in suppressing the
conspiracy of Edric Earl of Shrewsbury, for which,
as it is said, he was immediately rewarded with a
grant of all that Earl's forfeited estates.

How long the manor and lands of Baddesley continued in the hands of Mortemer and his descendants,
does not appear; neither has it yet been discovered,
when or by whom they were given to the Knights
Hospitallers.† It is however certain, that at a very

—whether both places might not, at some very distant time, have
belonged to one and the same person.

Jordanus de Clinton was one of the earliest benefactors to the
Commandry of Baddesley.—See Dugdale, Monast.

* See Peerage, vol. ii, part ii, p. 15.

† Dugdale says, that they first belonged to the Templars; and

early period they made a part of their property, and that they were considered of such value, as to be worthy to have a Commandry established upon them ; and the antient building some years since destroyed by fire, * but still remembered by many of the inhabitants by the name of the *Old Monastery,* was the residence of the Commander, and of the several members of his Society.

The origin of these Knights is very remote, this being the most ancient of all the military orders.† They were first associated in the year 1092, and were then distinguished by the appellation of "Knights of St. John of Jerusalem," but afterwards by that of *Knights Hospitallers ;* from an hospital which the founders of the Order built at Jerusalem, for the purpose of receiving the sick and indigent pilgrims, who came thither to visit the holy sepulchre. At their first institution, they were few, poor, and

that after the suppression of that Order, they were given to the Hospitallers, viz. in 1323 : but this is certainly a mistake; there being unquestionable evidence, that they had been in the possession of the Hospitallers, at least nineteen years before that time.

* The whole of the building was not destroyed, the kitchen having escaped with but little injury. This is now standing, and answers the same purpose to the present mansion-house, as it did to the Commandry ; for there can be no doubt, from its size and monastic appearance, but that it made a part of that ancient building.

In the manor farm-house some of the arms and military accoutrements of the Knights—such as swords and saddles—are still to be seen. Even now the latter are in pretty good preservation, and well deserve the notice of the curious.

† It seems to be a question undecided, which of the two Orders was the most ancient—whether that of the Hospitallers or the Templars. Vertot and Mosheim make the former, Camden and Jacob the latter, the oldest. I follow the two former writers as the best authorities.—See Mosheim, vol. 1, p. 559.—Burn Monasteries.

insignificant;* but being patronised by the rich
and great, they soon increased in number, and
arrived at great wealth and respectability: so that
at one time they possessed in the different king-
doms of Christendom, not fewer than nineteen
thousand lordships, or manors.†

The time of their first obtaining a settlement in
England, was about the year 1100; when a house
was built for them in or near London, by Jordan
Brisset, a wealthy citizen.‡ Here, says Camden,
they lived for some years, poor and humble; their
Governor styling himself " The Servant of the poor
Servants of the Hospital of Jerusalem." The piety
and superstitious notions of the age were, however,
soon the means of changing their circumstances:
For it appears, that within little more than a century, their house in London had, from a mean and
ordinary edifice, grown up to the stateliness of a
palace; and their Prior, or Superior, not only sat
among the Lords in Parliament, but was accounted
the first Lay Baron in the kingdom. §

In this prosperous condition, possessed of all the
wealth, as well as all the honours they could expect, or wish for, they continued to flourish till
the year 1541; when the Parliament, in obsequious
obedience to the King's suggestion, voted their
suppression, and placed the whole of their property at his disposal.¶ One, among other reasons

---

* All writers agree in this.
† See Camden Britannia, p. 321.
‡ Camden, as above, and Dugdale, Monast. Ang. p. 565.
§ Camden. Fuller, book vi, p. 294. Vertot, vol. ii, p. 61, folio.
¶ See stat. 32 Hen, VIII. chap. 24, sec, 1.

assigned for the expediency of this measure was,
that the Knights maintained the usurped power of
the Bishop of Rome; that is, as I suppose, his
supremacy. But though this might indeed be one
cause of their suppression, yet it is probable that
their tempting possessions was a still more powerful
motive to it; since, besides the superior house in
London, they had at this time no fewer than forty-
seven smaller houses subordinate to it, in different
parts of the country; and their revenues altogether
amounted to upwards of eight thousand pounds per
annum:* which, according to the present reduced
value of money, is equivalent to at least ten or
twelve times that sum now.

The *smaller* Houses just mentioned, were denominated Commandries; which in their design and
constitution, were exactly similar to those smaller
institutions of the Templars, called Preceptories;
that is, they were small societies of those Knights
placed upon some of their principal, or distant
manors, for the purpose of seeing them, and any
other smaller estates they might possess in the same
neighbourhood, properly managed. In all these
Societies the person who had the controul, was
styled, analagously to the name of the whole body,
Commander. But though he was the Superior
within his own House, he was nevertheless subject
to the authority of the Grand Prior in London;
and obliged, after defraying the expences of his

---

* Burn, vol. ii, 68.

own Society, to account for the remaining profits of the estate to him.*

When the House of this description was first instituted at North Baddesley,† is not known exactly; nor will it, I imagine, be easy now to ascertain. There is, however, unquestionable evidence, that it was established so early as in Edward the First's reign :‡ and, if we may judge from the number and great respectability of its benefactors§, and the value of the property they had bestowed upon it,¶ one of greater consideration was not perhaps to be found in the kingdom.

Out of the many persons who, during a period of nearly three centuries, must have filled the office of Commander of the Society, the only one whose name I can mention with certainty, was Sir William Weston.** He had been chosen to this situation

---

* Vertot, vol. ii, b. xiii, p. 125.

† Tanner says it was at *South* Baddesley that the Commandry was situated, and Mr. Warner and others, following him as their guide, without inquiry, have fallen into the same error.

‡ It appears by the registers of the diocese, that the Knights Hospitallers were in possession of the manor and lands of the parish in 1304. This was eight years before the suppression of the Templars, and nineteen before their property was given to the Hospitallers.

§ In the Catalogue of Benefactors, given by Dugdale, may be seen the names of Jordan de Clinton, Adam de Port, William de St. John, and many other equally renowned persons.

¶ The annual value of the estates belonging to the Commandry, as reported to Henry VIII. by the visitors, was 118*l*. 16*s*. 7*d*. but this was probably far short of their real value.

** See Record in possession of Sir Nathaniel Holland, Bart.

In the list given by Vertot of the Knights assembled in the Isle of Rhodes, for its defence against the Turks, in 1480, five are there mentioned as being of the language of England; of which number, Henry Haler, who is described as Commander of Badsfort, was one. Now as it is certain that there was no Commandry, nor any parish of

about the middle of the reign of Henry the Eighth, and was afterwards appointed by that King, Lord Prior of the Hospital of St. John ;---a station which he filled with the greatest credit, and no less prudence and 'circumspection than the circumstances of the times required. But prudence and circumspection could be no security to his Order, against the will of an arbitrary Monarch; nor, though he employed his interest and influence to the utmost, with every other expedient that zeal could suggest to save it, could he avert the danger that awaited it. Five years had now elapsed since the Religious Orders had been suppressed, and the King's wants were again become urgent; and no other means of supplying them remaining, but the property of the Hospital, its dissolution was of course inevitable. To the Lord Prior, as a compensation for his loss, a pension of a thousand pounds per annum was granted for life; but he lived not to receive a penny of it. Grief at the approaching fate of his House, it is probable, had preyed upon his spirits prior to its suppression, and made a wound which it was not within the reach of the King's bounty afterwards to heal; for he died on the very day on which the dissolution was decreed---" Soul-smitten with sorrow," says Fuller, " at hearing of that---to him---fatal disaster."*

---

this name, in this kingdom, it may be safely presumed, I think, that Vertot mistook the termination of the word, and that *Badsley,* not *Badsfort,* was the name of the place of which Henry Haler was Commander.—See Vertot, vol. 1, Proofs, p. 105.

* See Fuller's Church Hist. p. 345.

His tomb may now be seen in St. John's Church, Clerkenwell.

The property of all kinds which now fell into the King's hands, was of very considerable value; and had it been properly applied for the benefit of the community, to whose use it was directed by Parliament to be appropriated, much permanent good might have been done by it. But as it was, neither the public, nor the King himself, derived any real advantage from it; since it was no sooner in his possession, than we find it either lost at play, sold for a trifle, or else lavishly granted away to court favourites. *

The person to whom it is said the manor and lands of Baddesley were first given, was Sir Thomas Seymour, Knt. created at the commencement of Edward the Sixth's reign, Baron of Sudley. He was brother to Edward Seymour, Duke of Somerset, and to Jane Seymour, Queen to Henry the Eighth; through which connexion, it may be supposed, he obtained the grant of Baddesley; for it was given to him in the thirty-second year of Henry's reign, and the same in which the Knights were deprived of it. Being attainted of high treason, he was condemned by the Parliament to suffer death; and was beheaded accordingly in the year 1549, and his estates were at the same time for-

---

It is of marble, with his effigies, well cut in stone, lying upon it. A part only of the inscription now remains.—See Weaver's Funeral Monuments, p. 430, and Pennant's Survey of London.

* " It is certain, says Fuller, that in this age, small merits of " courtiers met with prodigious recompense for their service. Not " only all the cooks, but the meanest turn-broach in the King's " kitchen, did lick his fingers." He then proceeds to mention several instances of the King's shameful waste of abbey lands.—History of Abbeys, p. 336.

† see Tanner, Notitia Monastica, & stat. 32 Henry VIII.

feited to the king. As usual however in those times, these were soon again disposed of; and Sir Nicholas Throcmorton, Knt. was the person who it appears next obtained the grant of Baddesley.* But he was not, more fortunate than his predecessor, in keeping possession of it; for the King dying soon after, he was, in the course of the following reign, dispossessed, and the manor and lands were again restored to their former owners, the Knights Hospitallers.†

Upon the restoration of the Order, the Queen, says Vertot, nominated Sir Richard Sceley, (Shelly he means), a great favourite of hers, Lord Prior, and immediately despatched a messenger to Malta, to acquaint the Grand Master with her proceedings. Upon the receipt of the information, the Commander Montferrat was sent without delay to England, for the purpose of reinstating the Knights in their possessions; in accomplishing which, it is asserted by Vertot, that he found but little trouble. ‡ But there is reason certainly for suspecting that the business was not so easily affected as this historian would have it supposed: for though the Commander arrived in England not later than in 1555, yet, according to Fuller's account, the Lord Prior was not invested with the Cross till the 30th of November, in the year 1557: and then, not Sir Richard Shelly, but Sir Thomas

---

* Stat. 5, Edward VI.
† So says Turner, and refers to stat. 4 and 5 Philip and Mary.—See also Vertot, vol. ii, p. 156.
‡ See vol. ii, p. 160.

Tresham, was the person advanced to that high dignity.*

But another revolution was now near at hand. The Queen's health was at this time rapidly declining, and in the year following, she died, to the great mortification, as well as disappointment, of the Papists; all their measures for restoring and preserving their religious establishments, being by this event entirely frustrated.

Whether or not Sir Nicholas Throcmorton regained the Baddesley property, upon the final suppression of the Order under Elizabeth, I have not been able to discover; but as he was an active Statesman in the reign of Elizabeth, and much employed in her service, it seems not unlikely that he did recover it. Be this however as it may, it is evident that it could not have remained long in his possession; since it appears that a Mr. Forster was the owner of the estate in in 1580; though, how long he had possessed it before that time, is not known, any more than the means by which he obtained it. It seems however pretty certain, that he had been long resident in the parish, previous to the already mentioned year; and the probability is, that he had been in possession of the property of it during that time. Who Mr. Forster was, I have not been able to learn, but conclude, from the following curious verses, that he was a person of some note and respectability:

---

* Fuller's Church Hist. book vi, p. 357. Seymour's Survey of London.

Mr. Forster, of Badsley,	was a good man
Before the marriage	of Priests began.
For he was the first	that married a Nun,
For which he begat	a very rude son.
Their daughter Andrew	married Sir Willm. Barew.

These singular lines are copied from an old manuscript paper written before the year 1668, and containing much interesting information concerning the parishes of Hursley and Baddesley. The person who wrote it was Richard Morley, a man possessed of some considerable landed property in Hursley; and who, according to his own account, went to school at Baddesley, to Ralph Blenstone, Minister of that parish, in the year of the great hail-storm.* To the lines he has prefixed the following note or memorandum: " A proverb when " I was a boy." From them it may, I think, be inferred, that the lady whom Mr. Forster had married, had been in a convent---perhaps in the neighbouring Abbey of Romsey---and that the connexion was not considered as a lawful one, even though the monasteries were then all dissolved :† and it is not improbable but that it was the *rudeness*, or, as the word may perhaps be understood to signify, *extravagance* of his son, which occasioned the selling of his estate.

* 1582. Camden's Annals of the Reign of Elizabeth.

† The case of the poor nuns was truly pitiable. Though dispossessed of their houses, dispersed and deprived of support, they were nevertheless obliged to keep their vow of celibacy; a law having been enacted for the express purpose of prohibiting them from marrying; than which, a stronger proof of the cruelty, oppression, and inconsistency of Harry the Eighth's conduct, can scarcely be adduced.

M

It appears from the manuscript above alluded to, that Mr. Forster had a brother, whose Christian name was *Barrowe*, and who was remarkable in his day for an extraordinary dream he had, which was made the subject of a ballad. What the nature of the dream was, tradition does not say, and the ballad, I imagine, no longer exists to speak for itself. This Barrowe Forster, it seems probable, had an interest in the estate at Baddesley; because, when it was sold by his brother, an annuity of an hundred pounds per annum was charged upon it for him, which he enjoyed for many years. At length, however, he was tempted to sell it, for the consideration of 800 *l.* which proved a fortunate circumstance for his family, as he died within a few days afterwards. The person to whom Mr. Forster sold the estate, was

Sir Thomas Fleming, Knt. He was a Lawyer, and after passing through the offices of Solicitor General, and Lord Chief Baron of the Exchequer, in the reign of Elizabeth, was, in the 5th year of King James (viz. in 1607) appointed Lord Chief Justice of the Court of King's Bench.* When he purchased Baddesley does not appear: but it was not later than the year 1582, and there is reason for supposing that he did not keep it longer than till 1602; for having, about that time, an opportunity of buying the manor of North Stoneham, of the Earl of Southampton, he disposed of

---

* Noble says he was Lord Chief Justice in the reign of Elizabeth, but this is not a correct statement.—See Camden's Annals of King James, anno 1607.

his property at Baddesley, for the purpose, as it is believed, of paying for that he had bought at Stoneham.

John More, Esq. who now purchased Baddesley of Sir Thomas Fleming, was also a Lawyer, and a Serjeant at Law, having been called to that degree by King James, in the year 1614.* He appears to have been a man much respected, and possessed of very considerable property---as not only Baddesley belonged to him, but Chilworth, Skidmore Farm, Romsey and Timsbury Parsonages, and the Manor of Romsey. It is said that he lived at Baddesley many years, though it is evident that he did not relinquish the business of his profession; for he died on the Western Circuit, in the year 1620, and in the 59th of his age. His remains were brought to Baddesley and buried in the chancel, where a monument is erected to his memory.

Serjeant More left only one son, John More, Esq. who, at the time of his father's death, was a Student at Oxford, where within two years after, he was attacked by the small-pox, of which he died when only in the 20th year of his age. He left two sisters, who now became co-heiresses of their father's extensive property. Of these, the eldest, Dulcibella, married Samuel Dunch, Esq, of Pusey, in Berkshire, fifth son of Sir Edmund Dunch, of Little Wittenham, in the same county: the youngest, Ann, Edward Hooper, Esq. of Chilworth, Hants.

* Baker's Chronicle, p. 316.

In the division of Mr. More's property, Chilworth, Romsey Manor and Parsonage, with a moiety of Timsbury Parsonage, fell to the share of Mr. Hooper; Baddesley, and Skidmore Farm, with the other moiety of Timsbury Parsonage, to that of Mr. Dunch, who is therefore to be considered as the next proprietor of the manor of Baddesley.

The time when this division is supposed to have been made, was about the year 1623, after which Mr. Dunch appears to have resided principally at Baddesley, and to have been very attentive to his interests there. He seems indeed to have been, in all respects, a man of business; for he was an active Member of the Long Parliament, and of that chosen by order of Cromwell, in 1654. He was also one of the Visitors of the University of Oxford, and a Member of the Committee, appointed in 1653, for the Reformation of Abuses and administering of the Civil Power.* Like the other branches of his family, he was a zealous supporter of Oliver Cromwell's Government, with whom he was a great favourite, probably not more on account of the connexion subsisting between their families, than from the confidence he had in his fidelity and abilities. He survived the Restoration several years, dying in the year 1668, at the advanced age of 77. By his wife, who died a few years only before him, he left five daughters and one son, viz.

John Dunch, Esq. This gentleman married Ann, the youngest daughter of Richard Maijor, Esq.

---

* Dugdale's View of the Troubles, p. 406. Walker's Sufferings of the Clergy, p. 126.

of Hursley, from whom he received at his marriage one thousand pounds, and at the death of Mr. Maijor, a moiety of all his remaining disposable property. It is said that he resided at Hursley with his father-in-law, and there is reason for believing the report, as all his children, except the youngest, were born there. He did not, however, lead an idle life; for it appears that he was an active Magistrate, had a commission in the army, and served in several of the Protector's Parliaments. Upon the death of Mr. Maijor in 1660, he is supposed to have retired to Baddesley, and to have lived partly there, and partly with his father in Berkshire. It is probable that his health was in a declining state at the time of his father's death, for he survived him only ten days; the one dying on the 20th, and the other on the 30th of October, 1668. At the time these melancholy events happened, they were resident in Berkshire; from whence their remains were brought and interred on the same day, and in the same grave, in the chancel at Baddesley.

The children left by Mr. John Dunch, were four sons and four daughters; the eldest of whom, Maijor Dunch, Esq. succeeded to the family estates in Hampshire. At the time of his father's death, he was only seventeen years of age; but being then put under the care of an able tutor,* he attained

---

* This was Mr. Humphrey Gunter, who it appears resided at Baddesley, in the mansion-house, for several years after the death of Mr. Maijor Dunch—having perhaps resumed his character of tutor to his deceased pupil's son, Wharton Dunch.

to considerable eminence, both for learning and all
other liberal and virtuous accomplishments. When
about twenty-five years of age, he married Mar-
garet, the daughter of Philip Lord Wharton, but
died within a few years after, in the twenty-ninth
year of his age; and was buried at Pusey, in
Berkshire, in September 1679. * On the South
side of the tower, adjoining to the church of
Baddesley, are the arms of the Dunch family, em-
paling those of More, † with these initials, M. D.
and the following date, 1674: from whence I conclude, that this little edifice, which is evidently
modern when compared with the church, was
built by him.   His widow afterwards married Sir
Samuel Selyard, of Kent, Bart.; but not till after
the year 1686: as it appears by some books she
presented to the church in that year, that she
had not then changed her name.   By her marriage
with Mr. Dunch, she had three children; two
daughters and one son, viz. :

Wharton Dunch, Esq. who inherited his father's
property, and lived some years at Baddesley; but
died early in life, and left no children. It was
during his minority, that Mr. Robert Thorner inhabited the mansion-house at Baddesley.   This
gentleman is said to have been a Dissenter; but it
should seem, that he was by no means a rigid, or

---

* See Le Neve, Monumenta Anglicana.
† These are—sable, a chevron engrailed or, between three castles
triple-towered argent; for Dunch: and—ermine, on a chevron
sable, between three blackamore's heads proper, two swords, points
upwards, argent; for More.

an illiberal one. At any rate, he was a man of great piety and benevolence; as the Alms-houses at the entrance of Southampton, and many other charitable institutions, which were founded and endowed by him, sufficiently evince. He was married at Baddesley, on Christmas-day 1689; and died and was buried there in the church-yard, in the July following. Upon the decease of Mr. Wharton Dunch, his estates descended to his only surviving sister, Jane, married to Francis Keck, Esq. of Great Tew, in Oxfordshire; who, of course, now became in right of his wife, possessed of her family property; and, as it seems, occasionally resided at Baddesley. He died in 1728, leaving only one son, John Keck, Esq. of whom I only know that he survived his father but a few months; and that his widow afterwards married John Nicoll, Esq. who purchased the Baddesley estate of Anthony Keck, the heir of the above-mentioned John Keck.

Mr. Nicoll was a man of letters, as well as of property; and appears to have been much respected in the parish, where he is still remembered by a few of the old inhabitants. He always kept the mansion-house in his own occupation, and generally resided a part of the year in it. He died, as it is supposed, about the year 1749; leaving his only child, a daughter and a minor, to the care and guardianship of the Rev. Joshua Harrison, the Rector of the parish; who had long been his intimate friend and associate, and of whom it ought in justice to be said, that one more capable of the trust, or more faithful to it, could not have been selected. When of age, Miss Nicoll married James Brydges, Marquis of Caernarvon, afterwards Duke of Chandos, who of course became possessed of her large fortune: but of this, the estate at Baddesley made no part, her father having possessed only a life-interest in it, or else sold it, previous to his death, to Anthony Chute, Esq. by whose brother it was, about the year 1767, again sold to Thomas Dummer, Esq. of Cranbury; from whom it has devolved to the present possessor, Sir Nathaniel Holland, Bart.

North Baddesley Church.

Drawn & Etched by T. Fidlo.

THE CHURCH

OF

NORTH BADDESLEY.

This little building is situated upon the highest point of land in the parish to the North of the scite of the old Commandry, from which it stands not more than fifty, or at the most, sixty yards distant. It is evidently a very ancient structure, but when it was erected, is perhaps now impossible to be ascertained. Three hundred years old it undoubtedly must be, but this is certainly far short of its real age, and probably not much more than half of it. Like most other Norman-built parish churches, this at Baddesley consists of one aisle only; the length of which, including the chancel, measures sixty-two feet, and the breadth sixteen. Both church and chancel are nearly of the same height, and the ceiling of both is arched or circular; that of the latter being divided by the timbers of the roof into square compartments, the corners of which are ornamented with shields of a red colour, like those borne by the Knights Hospitallers. The little tower at the West end, was built in 1674. It is thirty feet high, and about five long by four wide in the inside, and has two ill-toned bells hanging in it.

At the entrance of the church, but on the outside

N

of the door, serving as a kind of step, is an old and much-worn stone, of the form here represented,

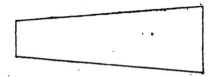

which there can be no doubt once covered the grave of some respectable person;* but as the foot, or smaller end of it, is now turned towards the West, it must have been displaced some time or other, though when and from whence is not likely ever to be known. On entering the church, the eye is at first attracted by an uncommonly large black stone lying on the ground in the middle of the aisle, the dimensions of which are eight feet three inches in length, by three feet nine inches in width. Upon this it is evident that a metal plate was originally fixed, with arms and inscription to commemorate the person whose remains it covers; but time has long since worn this away, and no judgment can be formed whose name it bore. There is, indeed, a notion in the parish that a Queen is buried underneath, but not the least reason whatever is assigned for the supposition, nor is there, in truth, the least foundation for it. It seems, however, not unlikely that one of the old Knights or Commanders may be

---

* Upon examining the surface of this stone, I have discovered, that the effigies of a person was originally affixed to it, the outline of the figure being still easily to be traced—from the form of which, compared with others of the same kind less injured, I judge the person it represented, to have been a Priest or Clergyman.

there deposited. Advancing towards the chancel, a stone, having the following inscription, makes a part of the pavement:

Hic jacet Reliquiæ
Magistri Thomæ Tompkins,
Theologi admodum reverendi
Hujus Ecclesiæ,
Nuper Pastoris vigilantissimi.
Qui obiit ,
Decimo nono die Junii,
Anno Domini 1702.

Nearly at the foot of this stone is a partition of open rail-work, dividing the church from the chancel, which, it is said, was erected by Sir Thomas Fleming; and the tradition seems confirmed by the initials of his name, and the year 1602 carved in the top of it.

Upon this partition are placed the King's arms. These, till newly painted in 1806, had the follow-ing names and date inscribed on the back of them:

John Forster, ⎫
John Browne, ⎭ Churchwardens, 1660.

As this was the year of the Restoration, it is supposed that the arms were at that time replaced in the church; since it may be considered as next to a certainty, that they were not suffered by the Dunches to remain there, during the usurpation of their friends, the Cromwells.

But the piece of antiquity most worthy of notice, is a small, but apparently very ancient tomb, standing in the chancel contiguous to the wall under the North window. It is of free-stone, rudely sculptured, with a covering of polished marble or granite, but without either name, or date, or inscription of any kind. At each end, is a large cross carved in the stone of the form here described:

and on the side, are crosses of the same description, but smaller; and arms and roses placed alternately. Of the bearings on the shield little more is now discernible than a bend dexter: but the cross is every where perfectly distinct, and is clearly the same as that borne by the Knights Hospitallers, or as they are now styled, " of Malta." Whose person this tomb contains or covers, is wholly unknown by the inhabitants, and undiscoverable by me; but I conclude that he was a Knight of the above-mentioned Order, and perhaps the person who bestowed the manor and lands of Baddesley upon it. It seems also not unlikely, from the place his tomb occupies in the church, that he was a benefactor to it, if not indeed in part the builder of it. A supposition this, which receives farther support from the circumstance, that in both the North and South windows of the chancel, there are arms of painted glass, which are undoubtedly the same as those upon the tomb. They are——party

per fesse, argent and gules; on a bend dexter or
three (2re.) of the first. It is true, that the bend
is the only charge discoverable in the arms on the
tomb; but this circumstance does not at all inva-
lidate the conjecture; since, in the present instance,
the bend is perhaps the only bearing capable of
being made discernible in coarse stone-work, and
where no colours are employed. Besides the arms,
there is on several panes of glass, in both the be-
fore-mentioned windows, the following character:

And in the upper corner of that to the North, on
the right hand, is another of this description:

This last character is evidently the Gothic letter T
formerly in use, and, as may be reasonably supposed, was intended in this place for the initial of
some person's surname. Originally there was, I
imagine, another of the same kind, in the left hand
corner; but this, judging from present appearances,

must have been long since broken. These characters and the arms, I have no doubt, have relation
to each other, and to the person buried under.
the tomb; but who this was, and when he lived,
there are not the means even of conjecturing.

Adjoining to the tomb just described, and indeed
partly supported by it, is a large monument erected
to the memory of John More, Serjeant at Law,
the inscription upon which is in the following
words;

Memoriæ

Johannis More, ad Legem servientis,
Viri consultissimi, integerrimi;
Et Johannis More, Armigeri,
Filii ejus unigeniti : Quorum,

Ille

Terrestris Fori Strepitus,
Cœlestis Chori Cantibus,
Die Augusti x v. Anno Salutis
1620, Ætatis suæ 59;

Hic

Ejusdem Mensis anno vertente 2do.
Suæ autem Ætatis 20;
Flos Juvenum, in Juventis Flore,
Tempus Æternitati
Commutavit.

Dulcibella et Anna, Gnatæ, Sorores,

Altera

Samueli Dunch, de Pusey,
In Agro Bercensi Armigero,

Altera

Edvardo Hooper, de Chilworth,
In Agro Southamptoniensi Armigero
Enupta,

Patris   Fratris

Pietatis ergô et Armoris,

Posuerunt.

En tua non constructa tibi Monumenta Viator :

Mori dum spectas Marmora, disce mori.

This monument is quite in the style of the age in which it was designed, extremely heavy and tasteless, and possessed of nothing observable, but its grotesque ornaments, and the play upon the word Mori at the end of the inscription ; which last, considering the puerility of such conceits at all times, had certainly been better avoided in this place.

Besides this monument, there are within the communion-rails, five large grave-stones lying on the ground, and covering the remains of as many persons of the More and Dunch families. There is also in the passage of the chancel, a fragment of an old grave-stone, on which the vestiges of a brass plate may be still seen: Nothing more, however, is discoverable, nor can any conjectures be formed concerning it.

The Church of North Baddesley is in the Deanry of Southampton, and the Benefice was anciently Rectorial and unconnected with any Order, either Religious or Military. It appears, however, to have been appropriated to the Hospital of St. John, soon after the establishment of the Commandry, though it still, as is evident from the registers of the Diocese, retained its original character of a Rectory. By Ecton it is called a Preceptory, but it may be questioned whether he or Dugdale, by whose authority he probably was guided, could have

assigned any good reason for so describing it, since
it is thought that it can never be made to appear to
have belonged to the Templars. The present description of the church is that of a *Donative*, which
is certainly its proper denomination; as when vacant,
it is filled by the mere gift alone of the Patron,
without either presentation, institution, or induction.
It is also, like other Donatives, exempt from the jurisdiction both of the Bishop and of the Archdeacon
of the Diocese; and the Minister is neither obliged
nor expected to undergo their visitations.* Indeed,
he has himself, the same as Incumbents of other free
churches, a right of jurisdiction within his own
parish; and it appears by the register of the
Peculiar,† that this right has not unfrequently
been exercised by him. The annual value of the
Benefice as rated in the year 1291, in what is
called Pope Nicholas's Valuation, was five pounds;
and for more than a century afterwards, it was as-
sessed at the same sum.‡ During this time, the
church was unquestionably endowed with the tithes
of the parish: but of these it seems, on some occasion or other, to have been deprived, a composition
in money having, in later times, been paid to the
Incumbent in lieu of them. At present, it is not
rated at all, neither is it liable to the payment of
any fees or ecclesiastical charges of any kind.

---

* See Burn, Article *Donative.*
† This book is now in the possession of Sir Nathaniel Holland,
Bart. the lord of the manor. It commences about the year 1700.
The Peculiar has also a seal belonging to it, the inscription round
which is as follows:—" Sigillum Regiæ Majestatis ad Causas Eccle-
" siasticas," and at the bottom of the arms—" Pro Peculiar'. Jur.
" Beatæ Mariæ de Baddesley. Ave Maria."
‡ Bishop's Registers.

Of the INCUMBENTS of the church I can give but an imperfect account, not having been able to discover even the names of many, who must at different, and not very distant times, have suc ; ceeded to the Benefice.

Martin de Lavington is the first whom I find mentioned. He was Rector in the year 1304.*

Richard Larcher, styled Acolitus, was collated by the Bishop of the diocese, in 1311, the right of appointment having lapsed to him through the patron's neglect.†

Thomas de Watford, on the presentation of William de Tottehale, Prior of the Hospital of St. John of Jerusalem, in England, was instituted Rector in 1313.‡

Galfridus de Tottehale, on the presentation of Richard de Panely, Prior of the Hospital of St. John of Jerusalem, was instituted Rector in 1317.§

Hugh de Alvestone, on the death of G. de Tottehale, was instituted Rector in 1367, on the presentation of John de Panely, Prior of the Hospital of St. John of Jerusalem.‖

John Welles, styled Presbyter, on the presentation of Brother Hildebrand Juge, locum-tenens of the Prior of the Hospital of St. John, &c. was instituted Rector in 1387.‖

William Wylnyghton, on the presentation of John Radynton, Prior of the Hospital of St. John, &c. was instituted Rector in 1393.‖

John Rusby, on the presentation of Brother Robert Nor-

---

* See Register of John de Pontissera, Bishop of Winton.
† Ibid.
‡ Register, Woodlocke, fol. 16.
§ Register, Sandale, fol. 18.
‖ See Register, Wykeham.

O

manton, locum-tenens Prioris, (ipso in remotis agente) was instituted Rector in 1399.*

Stephen Edwards, on the presentation of Walter Grendon, Prior of the Hospital of St. John, &c. was instituted Rector in 1402.*

William Burton, by exchange with Edwards for Northall in Essex, was instituted in 1403, on the presentation of the same Walter Grendon.*

John Bone, by exchange with Burton for Fisheton, was instituted Rector in 1407, the same Walter Grendon being still Prior and Patron.†

From this time no entry of any institution to the church of Baddesley could be found in the registers of the diocese.

The person whom I next find mentioned as Incumbent of the church was Ralph Blenstone. He was Rector in 1582, and, as it is recorded, " taught school," at that time, " in the room over the gate-way leading into the Old " Monastery." Who was his immediate successor is not known; neither indeed does it appear who were the Incumbents for nearly a century afterwards.

The name which first occurs after this interval, is that of Timothy Goodacre, who was Incumbent in 1680, from which time the succession has been as follows :—

Samuel Hardy, in possession in 1683.

Aaron Wood, in possession in 1685.

Thomas Tomkins, appointed in 1693. It is said that he was blind, but that he, nevertheless, performed the duties of his office with much credit to himself and satisfaction to his parishioners. He lies buried in the church, and the frame in which he placed the sand-glass, by which he regulated the time of his preaching, was, not long since, to be seen there.

John Raymond, appointed in 1702. He died in 1719, and is buried in the chancel.

---

* See Register, Wykeham.
† See Register, Beaufort.

William Raymond, brother of the foregoing, officiated as Minister of the parish till 1723, but, I believe, was not Incumbent.

Joshua Harrison, appointed not later than 1723. He was educated in Queen's College, Oxford, and was also Rector of West Titherley, where he died, and was buried in 1773, having been incumbent of Baddesley fifty years.

Rennel Cotton, appointed by Thomas Dummer, Esq. in 1773.

John Penton, appointed by the same Thomas Dummer, Esq. in 1779.

John Marsh, appointed by Sir Nathaniel Holland, Bart. in 1802.

THE REGISTER of the parish begins with the year 1682. The average number of baptisms from the year 1701 to 1720, inclusive, is about five to each year, and that of burials about three to a year. From 1741 to 1760, inclusive, the number of baptisms was 119, (nearly 6 to a year) and that of burials 81. In 1749, the number of burials was 20, from whence I conclude that the small-pox, or some other pestilential disease, then prevailed in the parish. Within the twenty years ending December 1800, the number of baptisms registered is only 68, and that of burials 30. But it is evident that the register was shamefully neglected during a part of this period, no entry having, for several years, been made in it. If a judgment may be formed from the last seven years, the population of the parish is now certainly increasing; the number of baptisms in that time amounting to 47, nearly seven to a year.

THE END.

CPSIA information can be obtained at www.ICGtesting.com
Printed in the USA
BVOW022322170613

323594BV00016B/570/P